Nightmarish Neighborhood #4

# Murders, Mysteries, and Myths of Sleepy Hollow, NY

by Eric Pleska

Write On Dudes
Productions

## CONTENTS

# DON'T BE SCARED, BE PREPARED

Proceed with caution. Although a fictional character from a legendary story appears on the cover of this book, the enclosed stories are all true and contain possibly disturbing details that will leave you questioning the thin line between reality and the supernatural. While rich in local offbeat history about Sleepy Hollow, NY, this nonfiction book also unveils tales of tragedy, century-old unsolved murders, and ghostly haunts.

Embark on a journey through time in the New York City suburb of Sleepy Hollow. Formerly known as North Tarrytown, this Westchester County village is a treasure trove of culture and history. As we traverse several hundred years, we'll encounter fascinating offbeat local historical figures, including an infamous pirate, a rumored conductor of the Underground Railroad, an eccentric hermit, the elusive Silent Pete, and some real-life people behind Sleepy Hollow's famous legendary story, including the Hessian soldier who lost his head during a nearby Revolutionary War skirmish.

Brace yourself for a bone-chilling journey into Sleepy Hollow's dark underbelly. If you're easily spooked, you might want to stop here. But if you're ready to uncover the spine-tingling history that hides beneath the seemingly pleasant, scenic suburban Hudson River village, then read on. This book is not for the faint of heart but for those who dare to explore the shadows.

# 1.) THE FIRST VICTIM

During the Revolutionary War, Westchester County became known as The Neutral Zone as it lay between the main headquarters of the opposing Patriot and British armies. As discussed in previous books of the Nightmarish Neighborhood series, this location made Westchester vulnerable to easy attacks by various organized groups of marauding looters, including the infamous DeLancey's Cowboys.

DeLancey's Cowboys were Loyalists led by James DeLancey, whose objective was to supply the British Army with cattle and supplies. The group consisted of several dozen skilled fighters on horseback, and their presence struck fear into the citizens of Westchester. However, in many instances, Cowboy raids were nothing more than glorified robberies of innocent farmers and families. These raids often involved torture, kidnapping, and even murder, which made the citizens live in constant terror.

The patriotic Martling family lived in Tarrytown at the corner of Franklin and White Streets since the early 1720s. Isaac's father, Abraham, served as a deacon at the Old Dutch Church of Sleepy Hollow, worked as a blacksmith, and was a justice of the peace. Isaac grew up at that house and, in 1759, enlisted in Captain Gilchrist's Company to fight in the French and Indian War, a conflict between the British and French over control of North America. He rose to the rank of sergeant, and despite losing an arm during a battle, he managed to return from the ordeal and live a reasonably normal life supporting the Patriot cause.

A contingent of DeLancey's Cowboys, led by one of James Delancey's right-hand-men, Nathaniel Underhill, raided Isaac Martling's Tarrytown farm in the 1770s. The posse of looters used quick hit-and-run tactics to poach all of Isaac's livestock, which they later sold for beef. Although this could have been the end of the story, Isaac Martling, driven by a deep sense of injustice, plotted his revenge.

Nathaniel Underhill, the hostile grandson of Captain John Underhill, the infamous Native American slayer responsible for savagely murdering hundreds of Siwanoy in Westchester, targeted Isaac's farm as retribution for a prior incident.

Isaac Martling was part of a Patriot mob, including members of the underground political organization, The Sons of Liberty, who arrested several influential Loyalists in Westchester. Among those arrested were a local judge, a Reverend, and Westchester's mayor, Nathaniel Underhill.

After being released from jail, Nathaniel sought revenge on the Patriots who had placed him there. The Sons of Liberty leader, Isaac Sears, had relocated to Massachusetts, so Nathaniel's target became Isaac Martling.

Isaac retaliated against Nathaniel's Cowboy raid on his farm by visiting Nathaniel's farm with a Patriot mob. They strung Nathaniel to a barn beam by his heels and force-fed him dry grain until he vomited. The feud between Isaac and Nathaniel could have ended there, but it didn't.

According to local lore, on May 26, 1779, Isaac met for a romantic rendezvous with a woman named Polly Katrina Buckhout. They met near a watering hole by the Martling house at the corner of White and Water Street. As the one-armed Isaac picked up a pail of water to return home, his nemesis, stalking his movements, sprung into attack.

With a group of Cowboys, Nathaniel ambushed Isaac from behind as Polly begged for mercy and fled. Nathaniel violently stabbed Isaac multiple times, mortally wounding him. Nathaniel, however, didn't stop there. With a sharp blade, Nathaniel brutally hacked Isaac's body into pieces and gruesomely severed his head.

The Cowboys then stormed into Martling's house, which a soldier frequently guarded during the war. Nathaniel and his colleagues surprised the guard, John Van Tassel. However, John challenged the enemy with his bayonet as they charged him.

As the scuffle ensued, Nathaniel saw a second soldier appear in the house doorway. Shots were fired, and the second soldier was on the ground.  John Van Tassel was soon surrounded, killed, and savagely hacked to pieces. Nathaniel and his posse of Cowboys approached the fallen second guard only to realize it was not a guard. It was Polly Buckhout wearing a man's hat. They had shot her dead.

Another version of the story is that a rifleman belonging to a roving group called Emmerich's Chasseurs shot Polly Buckhout, thinking she was an enemy soldier, though this rumor may have originated with Nathaniel Underhill to serve as a cover-up.

One-armed war veteran Isaac Martling became Tarrytown's first murder victim. He is buried in the cemetery of The Old Dutch Church with his severed head beside him. His epitaph reads, "Inhumanly slain by Nathaniel Underhill. May 26, 1779, in his 39th year."

The patriotic Requa family moved into the Martling house a year or so later.  Meanwhile, Colonel Aaron Burr took command of American forces in Westchester County and launched an attack on the DeLancey homestead. Lamp oil-filled fire bombs were launched at the home, followed by lit torches. Many of The Cowboys left town shortly after, including Nathaniel Underhill, who "found it convenient" to relocate to Nova Scotia, Canada. Years later, Isaac Martling's headstone became broken at the base and went missing. Some locals speculated it was the doing of remaining Cowboys that stayed in town.

# 2.) BEYOND THE LEGEND

Long before novelist Mark Twain purchased a colossal mansion in Tarrytown, and even over a century before J.D. Salinger wrote his famous novel *Catcher In The Rye* in a Tarrytown garage apartment, the village on the banks of the Hudson River was home to one of the most famous writers of the 19th century: Washington Irving.

Washington Irving's birth in early April 1783 in New York City coincided with the official ceasefire that ended the Revolutionary War. His mother named him after General George Washington, whom he had the great fortune to meet at the age of six during the President's inauguration.

The blessing that George Washington bestowed upon young Irving during this encounter was so significant that the Irving family commemorated it in a beautiful watercolor painting that hung in their home. Such a remarkable beginning to his life is a testament to the impact that Washington Irving would go on to have on American literature and culture.

Growing up in Manhattan, Irving was an uninterested student who preferred adventure stories and drama. He regularly snuck out of class in the evenings to attend the theater. In 1798, an outbreak of yellow fever in Manhattan prompted his family to send him upriver, where he stayed with his friend James Paulding in Tarrytown, NY. The small village in southern Westchester County is about 25 miles from midtown Manhattan. He quickly became familiar with neighboring North Tarrytown and fascinated with the Hudson Valley's local history.

In 1809, while grieving the death of his 17-year-old fiancé, Matilda Hoffman, 26-year-old Irving began writing his first major work, *A History of New York*, a satire of self-important local history and politics. Before the book's release, Irving played a prank.

 He placed ads in New York newspapers looking for information on a supposed missing man, Diedrich Knickerbocker, a grumpy Dutch historian who allegedly vanished from his hotel in New York City. As part of the hoax, Irving also published a notice from the hotel's proprietor, stating that if Mr. Knickerbocker failed to pay his outstanding bill, he would publish the manuscript that Knickerbocker had left behind.

 Readers eagerly followed Knickerbocker's story and manuscript with interest, and some city officials offered a reward for his safe return. On December 6, 1809, Irving published *A History of New York* under the pseudonym "Diedrich Knickerbocker," which became an immediate success and brought Irving fame.

 "Diedrich Knickerbocker" became a nickname for Manhattan residents and was later adopted by the New York Knickerbockers basketball team. New York City's nickname Gotham, later popularized by comic book hero Batman, also originated from Irving's writing.

Irving lived in England for a few years following the release of his book about New York and, while there, became instrumental in introducing Americans to the modern celebration of Christmas.

In the early 19th century, Americans did not widely celebrate Christmas in the United States. While in England, Irving became struck by the English custom of decorating homes with evergreens and lighting candles on Christmas Eve. He began writing about his experiences in England and described the Christmas celebrations he witnessed. In 1820, his story "Christmas Eve" took the wintertime holiday to new heights in the United States.

The story takes place in an English country manor, where friends invite the narrator to spend Christmas Eve with them. Irving fills the story with descriptions of holiday traditions, such as the Yule log, mistletoe, and Christmas carols. His vivid descriptions help create a romanticized Christmas image that captures readers' imaginations.

Irving's influence on Christmas didn't stop there. In 1822, he published a poem called "The Children's Friend," which introduced the character of Santa Claus to American audiences. The poem describes Santa Claus as a jolly, rotund man who travels in a sleigh pulled by reindeer and delivers gifts to children on Christmas Eve. He based the character on the Dutch figure of Sinterklaas, but Irving's poem helped to popularize the image of Santa Claus that we know today.

Another of Irving's Christmas stories, "The Crayon Papers," features Squire Bracebridge, a character who hosts a Christmas celebration at his country estate. He packed the story with descriptions of holiday traditions, such as the Christmas feast, the burning of the Yule log, and the singing of carols. Irving's writing helped to create a sense of nostalgia for a simpler time when Christmas was a time of family, friends, and good cheer.

Despite Irving helping to mold the way America's most popular holiday is celebrated and inadvertently naming an NBA franchise, perhaps his most well-known work and character come from his 1820 collection of 34 short stories, *The Sketchbook of Geoffrey Crayon*. Within the book, which also contains the short story "Rip Van Winkle," is the iconic "The Legend of Sleepy Hollow."

Irving's tale of a small-town school teacher, Ichabod Crane, and the Headless Horseman is perhaps America's first ghost story.

The story's text purports to have been discovered "among the papers of the late Diedrich Knickerbocker." The tale is set in 1790 in the countryside near the former Dutch settlement of Tarrytown, in a secluded glen known as Sleepy Hollow.

The story is about Ichabod Crane, a tall, skinny, and superstitious teacher from Connecticut who teaches the children of Sleepy Hollow in exchange for room and board. He plans to win the heart of Katrina Van Tassel, the daughter of a wealthy farmer, to get access to her family's riches. However, he has to compete with Brom Bones, the town's rowdy troublemaker, who is also interested in Katrina. As Ichabod is not willing to fight for Katrina's love, Brom starts playing pranks on him to make his life difficult.

Ichabod is invited to a harvest party at the Van Tassel homestead one autumn night. He dances, partakes in the feast, and listens to ghost stories other partygoers tell. In particular, Brom tells how he once raced against the Headless Horseman of Sleepy Hollow, the notorious ghost of a Hessian trooper decapitated by a cannonball during the Revolutionary War. The Horseman is supposedly buried in a churchyard in Sleepy Hollow and rises from his grave every night to search for his missing head, but is supernaturally barred from crossing a wooden bridge that spans a nearby stream.

Ichabod propositions Katrina, but she rejects his advances. He leaves the party heartbroken and rides home on a temperamental plow horse named Gunpowder. It is the witching hour, and with his mind preoccupied by the evening's ghost stories, Ichabod sees ghouls and goblins at every turn. He encounters a cloaked rider upon a black horse and - on spotting the rider carrying his head atop his saddle - recognizes him as the Headless Horseman. Ichabod rides for his life, desperately spurring Gunpowder down the Hollow. The Horseman gives chase and pursues Ichabod to the wooden bridge, where he suddenly rears back and throws his severed head, knocking Ichabod off his horse.

The next morning, Gunpowder is found grazing at his master's gate. There's no sign of Ichabod except for his discarded hat and the remains of a shattered pumpkin. With his romantic rival missing and presumed dead, Brom marries Katrina. The true nature of the "Headless Horseman" remains a mystery, but it's hinted that it might have been Brom all along, playing yet another malicious prank on Ichabod. Whenever the story of Ichabod's disappearance is told, Brom is said to "look exceedingly knowing" and always laughs heartily at the mention of the broken pumpkin.

Years later, a local farmer returns from a visit to New York and reports that Ichabod is alive and well. Humiliated by Katrina's rejection and frightened by his encounter with the Headless Horseman, Ichabod fled Sleepy Hollow, moved to "a distant part of the country," studied law, entered politics, and eventually became a judge.

However, according to the old Dutch wives of Tarrytown, Ichabod was "spirited away" by the Headless Horseman. Following his disappearance, Ichabod's schoolhouse was abandoned, forcing his students to relocate to another school. According to legend, Ichabod's voice haunts the abandoned schoolhouse, and on quiet summer evenings, his ghostly voice can be heard chanting a melancholy psalm tune at a distance among the tranquil solitudes of Sleepy Hollow.

Although "The Legend of Sleepy Hollow" by Washington Irving is a fictional story, some of its characters, such as Brom Bones and Katrina Van Tassel, as well as its locations, are thought to be inspired by real people, places, and historical events from the region.

The story mentions multiple real-life locations, such as The Old Dutch Burial Ground, Wiley's Swamp, Raven's Rock, and where three local men apprehended British spy Major John Andre during the Revolutionary War.

Local tradition is that the flirty Katrina Van Tassel character was associated with the local Revolutionary War-era tavern, The Elizabeth

Van Tassel House. According to historian Edgar Mayhew Bacon, in his 1898 book Chronicles of Tarrytown and Sleepy Hollow, Irving was a frequent visitor to the Van Tassel House.

The tavern once stood at what is now the northeast corner of Hamilton Place and North Broadway in Tarrytown. It was the location of the Washington Irving School, which opened in 1897 and was later renamed the Franklin Pierce School in 1920 after the town opened a new nearby school bearing Irving's name.

While perhaps Irving based his famous female lead character on the name of a local tavern, it may be worth pointing out that Irving enjoyed reading about the Revolutionary War and regional history. Irving references a local Revolutionary War skirmish when describing the Headless Horseman and mentions the real-life capture of Major John Andre in Tarrytown.

Therefore, despite what some local historians may believe, it's perhaps more likely that Irving's basis came from a mixture of Tarrytown murder victims, Polly Katrina Buckhout and John Van Tassel. Adding to this theory is that Tarrytown's first murder victim, Isaac Marling, was survived by a sister and brother. Sister Elizabeth married a local militiaman named Jacob Buckhout. Brother Abraham Martling Jr. worked as a blacksmith, rode a big black horse, and was known to friends by his nickname, Brom.

The Headless Horseman is perhaps America's earliest and most well-known ghostly phantom. As described by Irving:

*"It is said by some to be the ghost of a Hessian trooper, whose head had been carried away by cannonball in some nameless battle during the Revolutionary War. Having been buried in the churchyard, the ghost rides forth to the scene of battle in nightly quest of his head."*

It's believed that Washington Irving drew inspiration for his Headless Horseman character from a gruesome event in White Plains during the Revolutionary War.

As previously discussed in *Nightmarish Neighborhood #3: Buckout Road*, in the days following the Battle of White Plains in 1776, General William Heath of the Continental Army headquartered on Hall Avenue, the street that turns into Buckout Road. While staying at the home of the patriotic Gilbert Hatfield, General Heath transcribed a journal entry about a nearby event that happened on Halloween night.

*"Here, unknown to them, were some 12-pounders, upon the discharge of which they made off with their field pieces as fast as their horses could draw them. A shot from the American cannon at this place took off the head of a Hessian artilleryman. They also left one of the artillery horses dead on the field. What other loss they sustained was not known."*

The event he's describing is when British soldiers and Hessian horsemen attempted to raid one of General George Washington's supply depots located at John Horton's Gristmill around the corner from Buckout Road on Lake Street.

General Washington used the cloak of a Halloween night rainstorm to stealthily move significant components of the Continental Army from various points of White Plains to nearby Wright's Mill at the site of the modern-day Kensico Dam Plaza. He left several key contingents of his army in White Plains, defensively stationed on hills to track the British Army's movements.

To the surprise of the would-be-supply-depot-raiders, Lieutenant Ephraim Fenno and other Patriots remained stationed overlooking Lake Street, about a quarter mile from the supply depot on Merritt Hill. Lt. Fenno fired his cannon at the approaching enemy, causing the British soldiers to retreat. However, the cannonball directly hit a Hessian warrior, blowing off his head.

The soldier, who some believe was a Grenadier under the command of Regiment von Rall, instantly died. His comrades carried him on horseback to his burial site in Sleepy Hollow. The whereabouts of his decapitated head remain a mystery.

Irving wrote: *"Having been buried in the churchyard, the ghost rides forth to the scene of battle in nightly quest of his head."*

Some believe the remains of the true Headless Horseman are in the Sleepy Hollow Cemetery in a grave marked "Hessian Soldier." According to legend, local history buff Irving first read about the Merritt Hill incident in 1799 at the Tarrytown library, less than half a mile from North Tarrytown, which, in 1996, was renamed Sleepy Hollow.

Washington Irving lived in an exquisite estate named Sunnyside for nearly twenty years in Tarrytown. He died there peacefully on November 28, 1859, at age 76. Afterward, he was buried in Sleepy

Hollow Cemetery, a short walking distance from the possible grave of the man behind his iconic short story Headless Horseman.

Despite Irving's death, his presence is said to still linger in the halls of Sunnyside. Some visitors insist that his ghost haunts the house to this day, making appearances to visitors and residents alike. Many have reported strange occurrences such as doors opening and closing on their own, footsteps heard in empty rooms, and a phantom figure glimpsed in mirrors or windows.

Some believe Irving's spirit remains at Sunnyside because he loved the house so much. Irving himself once wrote of the property, "I have a snug little cottage...which I hold in high estimation for its picturesque beauty and its retirement." This deep affection for his home underscores the emotional connection Irving had with Sunnyside, perhaps explaining why his spirit is believed to still reside there.

Regardless of the reason for his continued presence, Washington Irving's legacy seems to live on not only in his literary works but also in the home where he spent his final years.

Irving's legendary tale has been adapted to a variety of movies, including Disney's animated *The Adventures of Ichabod and Mr. Toad* in 1949, Tim Burton's 1999 gothic version starring Johnny Depp, and *The Smurfs: The Legend of Smurfy Hallow* in 2013, the same year that Fox debuted its supernatural drama series *Sleepy Hollow* which aired 62 episodes and featured footage filmed in Sleepy Hollow, NY.

# 3.) MAJOR ANDRE'S CAPTURE

The capture of Major John Andre in Tarrytown, NY, has been told and retold for over two centuries. It is a story of espionage, betrayal, and the consequences of war. But what many people don't know is that the story doesn't end with Andre's execution.

As discussed in *Nightmarish Neighborhood #1- The Lost Village Of Kensico*, during the Revolutionary War-era world of 1780, British spy John Andre secretly met with General Benedict Arnold, who had recently defected from the American to the British side of the war.

During their secret meeting off the coast of the Hudson River in Rockland County, NY, General Arnold gave Major Andre classified documents that he could use to help the British take over America's fort at West Point, NY, which Arnold was in command of.

The fort at West Point, located on a hill above a narrow bend of the Hudson River, was the critical military site for defending the waterway. The British believed that control of the Hudson River would isolate New England from the rest of the colonies and cause the patriotic rebellion to fail.

At the time, John Andre was 30 years old and very well-liked amongst peers in colonial society. He was a prolific writer, singer, and well-versed artist known for his unique paintings and silhouette drawings.

He was fluent in multiple languages, including English, French, German, and Italian, and had recently been promoted to take charge of the British Secret Service in America.

Andre arrived to meet Arnold on a boat, Vulture, and planned on returning to it to travel safely back to British territory after their meeting. However, during their meeting, several patriots attacked Vulture, causing it to flee the area and leave Andre abandoned.

Now, Andre's secret mission had become a high-stakes dance of deception and danger. To avoid arrest, he had to navigate through enemy territory on horseback, cross the treacherous Hudson River, and elude American patrols.

General Arnold gave him traveling instructions, which included staying inland, swapping his British military uniform for civilian clothes, and a phony passport with the alias "John Anderson."

Unfortunately for Andre, after he crossed the eastern side of the Hudson River at King's Ferry, he didn't continue his journey by keeping inland as Arnold instructed. Instead, Andre shifted west until he was riding down the Albany Post Road, which follows the edge of the Hudson. He rode safely until 9 am on September 23rd, shortly after crossing a stream called Clark's Kill, later renamed Andre River, on the border between Tarrytown and Sleepy Hollow.

Westchester farmers John Paulding, Isaac Van Wart, and David Williams joined the local militia to defend their families and homes.

While patrolling Tarrytown, they saw Andre, found him suspicious, and stopped him.

Andre allegedly believed the militiamen were Loyalists because Paudling was wearing a Hessian soldier's coat. Unbeknownst to Andre, he only had the coat because the day before, he had escaped from a British prison with the help of a sympathetic Loyalist who provided him with it to aid in his escape.

 Assuming he was amongst allies, Andre told the three men he was a British officer who must not be detained. Paulding responded by telling Andre they were Americans and were placing him under arrest. Andre then pivoted and tried to convince them he was actually an American officer. In perhaps the first case of a fake I.D. used in Westchester, Andre displayed the phony passport given to him by General Arnold.

 The militiamen weren't convinced the odd man on horseback was really "John Anderson" and searched him. They found Arnold's papers and the plans for West Point hidden in his stocking. Andre offered them his horse and watch to let him go, but they declined.

 They took Andre to be questioned by authorities at the Continental Army base at Wright's Mills, later named the village of Kensico. Colonel Jameson detained Andre in Reuben Wright's barn.

 After several rounds of questioning by various officers, including by General Washington's Culper Spy Ring leader Benjamin Tallmadge, Andre and Arnold's plan unraveled.

Andre asked Tallmadge how General Washington would treat him. Tallmadge responded by telling Andre that he had been a Yale classmate of American spy Nathan Hale, whom the British had captured and executed by hanging, in what Tallmadge described as a cold-blooded execution.

Patriots transported Andre to Tappan, NY where he awaited trial. Sir Henry Clinton tried to save Andre by writing to George Washington. However, Washington would only agree to a prisoner exchange involving Benedict Arnold, which the British declined.

The court found Andre guilty and sentenced him to death by hanging. Despite Andre's crimes, some American officers, including Alexander Hamilton, lamented his death sentence. A day before his hanging, Andre drew a self-portrait of himself with pen and ink, which Yale College now owns.

On October 2, 1780, Major John Andre placed the noose around his neck and tightened it himself. Reports said some who attended Andre's hanging, including Marquis de Lafayette, wept. A religious poem Andre had written a few days prior was found in his pocket after his execution.

More than 40 years after John Andre's death, in 1821, the Duke of York successfully arranged for the exhumation of his remains and transported them back to England to be interred at Westminster Abbey. Around 1879, American businessman Cyrus W. Field erected a granite monument to commemorate the site.

Locally, after Andre's hanging, the United States Congress gave each of Andre's captors, Paulding, Van Wart, and Williams, a silver medal known as the Fidelity Medallion and a pension of $200 per year, which came close to the annual pay of a Continental Army infantry ensign at the time.

A gigantic tree, now commonly called the Major Andre Tree, is believed to have been on the road where the militiamen apprehended Major John Andre. Washington Irving mentions the tree several times in his legendary tale about Sleepy Hollow, including it being the location where Ichabod Crane is attacked by the Headless Horseman. It's said that Andre's ghost haunts the towering tree, whose branches seem to reach for the sky.

In 1801, news spread to Tarrytown that the man, perhaps forever linked to John Andre, Benedict Arnold, had died. While locals rejoiced at the death of the American traitor, the sky burst into a terrorizing storm, producing roaring thunder and gigantic bolts of lightning.

After the storm cleared away, Andre's tree, under which three local Patriots had seized the treacherous documents from Benedict Arnold years prior, was splintered by lightning.

Some believe that on moonlit nights, a figure dressed in a British military uniform materializes near the site of the former iconic tree. This spectral figure, believed to be Andre, is said to wander around, forever searching for his lost documents. For generations, locals have claimed to hear the ghostly footsteps of a horse, adding to the enigma of his haunting presence. Some even claim to have seen the mysterious figure vanish into thin air, leaving only a chill in the night air.

Despite no concrete evidence to support the existence of Andre's ghost, the legend has persisted for over two centuries. It reminds us of the tragic consequences of war and the lasting impact it can have on a place and its people.

About 200 yards from the tree, a small brook crossed the road and ran into a marshy and thickly wooded glen known as Wiley's Swamp. A few rough logs made up a wooden bridge, known as The Horseman's Bridge, referred to in Irving's tale as the bridge where The Headless Horseman struck Ichabod Crane with a pumpkin.

During the 1800s, the wooden structure described by Irving was demolished. In 1929, the Westchester County Board of Supervisors unanimously decided to rebuild the legendary bridge, carrying Broadway over the Pocantico River, on the west side of the Old Dutch Church.

The site of the notorious Major Andre tree was inside a 4-acre park designed in 1892, Patriot's Park. In 1853, a bronze statue of John Paulding was added near the park and commentated with a large parade and dedication ceremony.

In 1982, Patriots Park, located on U.S. Route 9, also called Broadway, along the boundary between Tarrytown and Sleepy Hollow, was added to the National Register of Historic Places.

# 4.) THE MAD MURDERER

The Sleepy Hollow community's sense of patriotism became so enormous following Major John Andre's capture that parents began naming their children after the militiamen who apprehended the British spy. This popular tradition was the case with a member of one of Westchester's oldest and most prominent families, the Buckhouts.

The family can be traced back to Dutch origins, with Jan Buckhout being the first to sail from Holland to America in the 1600s. Jan's grandson, Captain Johannes Buckhout, served as a militia captain supporting the Continental Army and lived to be 103 years old. According to his headstone in Sleepy Hollow's Old Dutch Burying Ground, "he left behind when he died, 240 children and grandchildren."

One of his descendants, Isaac Van Wart Buckhout, was born on January 22, 1833. Isaac's parents gave him the middle name Van Wart in honor of Isaac Van Wart, one of the militiamen who arrested Major John Andre, who was also related to the Buckhout family through marriage. Patriot Isaac Van Wart was the brother of Isaac Van Wart Buckhout's matriarchal grandmother.

Isaac's father, Stephen, was a prominent Quaker and moved the family from Chappaqua to Ossining in 1838. Isaac grew up as a clumsy kid who enjoyed lounging around the village in the company of the most vicious troublemakers as an adolescent. He seldom went to school and was quite unruly when he did attend. Consequently, he grew up with no literary attainments or refinement.

As he got older, he briefly worked as a country store clerk with his brother Benjamin. Soon after, he decided to go into business for himself by opening a coal yard after taking a loan from his parents. He lost about $10,000, which is worth approximately $400,000 today.

In 1858, Isaac became romantically involved with a girl from Tarrytown named Anna Louisa Coupe. She was 20 years old and came from a wealthy and respected family. The young couple soon eloped.

Isaac's father-in-law got him a job at his wood and coal business, but it didn't pan out. Isaac's brother Benjamin tried to employ him, but Isaac had no interest. Instead, he enjoyed hunting and playing the violin.

In 1864, Anna purchased a 60-acre farm in Sleepy Hollow. Isaac, however, soon let it go to ruin. Around this time, he also got into some trouble for allegedly seducing the young daughter of their neighbor, Francis Weeks.

Another neighbor, Alfred Rendall, interceded and helped settle things between Isaac and Mr. Weeks. Isaac, who had fled the area to avoid troubles with Mr. Weeks, was permitted to return home safely without fear of any issues after paying Weeks a $500 fee.

While away from home, Isaac stayed with a friend named Willet Brown, who lived about three miles away. Willet later commented that he would often walk in and find Isaac talking and laughing to himself without explanation.

Again, Alfred Rendall interceded, and after a six week absence, Isaac returned home but was moody and ill-humored, so much so that Anna became afraid of him.

Shortly after, Isaac began circulating stories that his wife, Anna, was unfaithful. Though unfounded, he suspected his wife was having numerous affairs with various men, including a local man named Dick Hillyer, who the Buckhouts met in 1869 and hired to dig a well on their property.

Part of Dick Hillyer's payment was a place to sleep that evening. Mrs. Buckhout prepared an area near the foot of the stairs near their bedroom. With a sick feeling in his stomach, Isaac was hardly asleep when he heard his wife leave their bed and join Dick for a while before sneaking back to the bedroom.

Isaac claimed:

*"She came in stealthily, closed the door quietly, and softly crept to my side. I suspected all the time where she had been. I did not make any accusation against her that night, but I examined Hillyer's bed the next morning. I knew my wife's physical condition then; I found indisputable evidence of the correctness of my suspicions. Afterward, when we three*

*were face to face, guilt was so strongly written upon their countenances that they were forced to admit their crime. She has been guilty of adultery with the lowest, dirtiest, meanest loafers in my town."*

Despite Anna denying the allegations, Isaac didn't believe her but distracted himself by hanging out with his neighbor, Alfred Rendall, whose family's new farm adjoined his and Anna's property.

Alfred was wealthy from his successful wine and liquor business and had recently moved to Sleepy Hollow from New York City with his wife Sara, daughters Lizzie and Marion, and 25-year-old son Charles. Alfred was about 20 years older than Isaac, and the pair enjoyed hunting and fishing together. However, over time, Isaac began to suspect his wife is also having an affair with Alfred.

Isaac confronted Anna about having an affair with Alfred, but she denied his baseless allegations. Despite Isaac's animosity, he agreed for the couple to join the Rendalls at their home to celebrate Christmas.

On Christmas Day 1869, Isaac and Anna had dinner with the Rendalls and enjoyed playing cards together. That is until Isaac began making accusations of cheating, which turned into an argument, culminating in Isaac storming out.

The next day, Lizzie Rendall visited the Buckhout house. Isaac was still angry and kept repeating things Alfred had said the night before, especially the line, "Ike, you and I are both worthless fellows, but we have good wives." Lizzie assured Isaac that her dad meant nothing mean-spirited. Isaac told Lizzie to ask her father and brother to come over and visit on New Year's Day.

Isaac saw Marion Rendall a couple of days later and told her the same thing he had told her sister, "tell your brother and father to come over and visit with us on New Year's Day."

A few days later, on New Year's Eve, the neighborhood butcher, John Kipp, dropped some meat off at the Buckhout house. While there, Mrs. Buckhout conversed with neighbor Ira Miller in the kitchen. She asked if he thought her husband had been acting strangely lately.

Isaac jumped up defensively and said, "What do you think me crazy? It does not run in the family to be crazy."

Isaac left the room and returned with a pistol. Ann asked him to put it away, but he refused. He turned and said, "I wonder what is going on down in the Hollow. The sheriff is after me." Isaac then said that last night, he dreamed he was in jail.

Early the following morning, Isaac Yerks, a worker on the Buckhout farm, rushed to investigate the sound of gunshots to ensure everyone was safe. He found Isaac Buckhout holding a gun. Isaac said he was trying to shoot a hawk but missed.

At 11 am that morning, Alfred Rendall and his son Charles were guests at the Buckhout home. Alfred sat in a chair with his back to the kitchen while Charles got comfortable on the sofa in the corner of the room. Mrs. Buckhout was in the kitchen, standing between a table and the stove, cooking a goose.

Isaac excused himself and returned with a pitcher of cider and glass goblets for their guests. He poured each of them a full glass, strangely not pouring a glass for himself. He told his guests to "drink heartily" before excusing himself to the bedroom.

He returned moments later with a shotgun.

Without saying a word, Isaac fired his loaded double-barreled shotgun at Alfred from close range. The charge struck Alfred's neck, killing him instantly as his son Charles, seated a few feet away on the sofa, watched in horror.

Isaac swung around and fired a shot at Charles. The blast partially struck the goblet of cider in Charles' hands and partially in his eye. Glass shattered with pieces embedded in his eyes and forehead. The shot entirely destroyed one of Charles' eyes, leaving him disfigured with an empty eye socket and soaked in blood.

Thinking Charles was dead, Isaac proceeded into the adjoining kitchen where his wife was preparing a goose, startled by the commotion. The 6-foot-tall and stocky Isaac immediately grasped the empty weapon by the stock, raised it above his head, and dealt a powerful blow, knocking Anna to the kitchen floor. He crushed her skull with such force that the gun broke, leaving three incised wounds caused by the gun's triggers.

Anna was left dying on the kitchen floor as her husband, her assailant, fled the gruesome scene and sprinted down the street to his neighbor Ira Miller's house, where Ira says he confessed to the crime, saying, "I surrender myself, I'm a ruined man."

Neighbor Mary Weeks saw Isaac flee from the house around noon. Her husband Francis went to investigate. He discovered the carnage at the Buckhout house and called for help.

Elizabeth Yerks, who worked on the Buckhout farm with her husband Isaac Yerks and his brother Ezra, was next to arrive, followed by a neighbor named William Campbell. They saw Charles Rendall on the sofa crying for help and Mrs. Buckhout lying on the kitchen floor, fighting to stay alive. Moments later, she died.

Dr. James Scribner arrived soon after and tended to the lone survivor of the massacre, Charles. Despite losing one of his eyes and part of an ear, after three days of being unconscious, he recovered.

Meanwhile, Ira Miller harnessed a team of horses and brought Isaac Buckhout to Tarrytown in a wagon. They arrived at the house of Constable Lawrence, who put Isaac in handcuffs and placed him in the White Plains jail. The following day, newspapers dubbed Isaac "The Mad Murderer of Sleepy Hollow."

As the Rendall family buried Alfred in Sleepy Hollow Cemetery on January 5, 1870, a newspaper interviewed Isaac from his White Plains jail cell.

*"My wife has wonderfully, shamefully wronged me. She was a heartless, bad woman. Her improper conduct has been the cause of my having frequently left her, and I have been induced only by the urgent solicitation of my neighbors ever to return to her."*

On January 14, 1870, while detained in White Plains awaiting trial, Isaac attempted suicide in his cell after reportedly seeing the apparition of his wife. Guards saved him, and his trial began a few weeks later on March 23rd.

Isaac's prominent family and wealth of friends began circulating stories that Anna had been unfaithful to him. They ensured he had the best legal team available, which included Francis Larkin, former judge W.H. Robertson. J.S. Millar, and Jackson Hyatt. The trial was a highly profiled news story covered daily by the local newspapers.

There was some controversy about whether or not Isaac was sane or suffering from a severe mental illness. Some testimonies explained Isaac had acted strangely for several days and was acting in a paranoid state. He allegedly stood near a window at times while holding a gun, insistent that the sheriff was after him. Others testified that Isaac heavily drank alcohol.

While Isaac's demeanor was quiet and careless, The Yerks family was horrified to be part of a murder investigation. Elizabeth Yerks even fainted while testifying in court. Her husband Isaac Yerks, who also worked on the Buckhout farm, testified:

*"The night before New Year's, I saw him by the store and spoke to him. He seemed depressed. I thought he acted irrationally. His gun was usually in the sitting room and sometimes in the kitchen. I never saw it in the bedroom. He was often in the barn and around the wagon house."*

Both daughters of the murdered Alfred Rendall testified, as did the disfigured Charles Rendall, who was still recovering from injuries sustained during the attack. Charles told the court that Isaac had previously accused one of his friends of having an affair with his wife a few weeks before New Year's.

A gentleman who worked on the Buckhout's farm for six weeks named Charles McCabe testified that Isaac:

*"was always imagining that someone wanted to kill him, at times he was sullen and sober, at other times wild and on one occasion remarked that the sheriff was after him to rob and kill him."*

Ira Miller's testimony included that he remembered Isaac falling off a wagon two or three years prior and complaining about his head hurting. Ira's relative Chase E. Miller testified that he remembered Isaac telling him he loved a young woman residing in his neighborhood more than his wife and that he drank heavily at times.

After ten days, the trial ended in a mistrial, with eight votes for a conviction and four for an acquittal on the grounds of insanity. Rumors began to circulate around the city about jury tampering.

While confined in the White Plains jail awaiting his subsequent trial, Isaac refused to speak to anyone, including his counsel. After a few days, the police administered a test involving chloroform. It's unclear what occurred, but they concluded that Isaac's "insanity" was an act.

Several doctors who interviewed Isaac in the county jail testified that he thought Westchester County was under Masonic control and that the

Freemasons were "out to get him." They described Isaac as having a peculiar appearance with a consistent blank expression.

Isaac's second trial for the murders of his wife and neighbor began a year later, in March 1871. Several medical experts testified that the accused killer belonged to a class of the most dangerous types of lunatics and should be institutionalized. Witnesses testified that Isaac would speak of his deceased mother as if she was still alive. Police officers said Isaac claimed to hear voices while confined to his jail cell.

Despite the testimonies and incriminating evidence, his second trial ended much like his first one, with an undecided jury.

Isaac Buckhout's third murder trial began in July 1871 in White Plains. The jury found him guilty of murder in the first degree with a recommendation for mercy. Judge Barnard sentenced Isaac to death by hanging.

The Governor of New York became involved and asked medical experts to examine Isaac to verify his sanity. After 15 days, the experts pronounced him sane, and Judge Barnard announced the execution would take place on Friday, September 1, 1871, in White Plains.

A month later, Isaac was playfully skipping along the corridor on return to his cell. In an interview, he stated:

*"I've discovered an affinity within the prison walls that did much to render his existence happier than it had been, and in case of being*

*assigned to a cell elsewhere for the rest of his life, would be with him there to soothe him and continue to be a sort of ministering angel."*

Isaac's counsel appealed the judge's verdict, which delayed his scheduled execution until February 16, 1872.

Due to the high-profile nature of the crime and its subsequent trials, Westchester residents were eager to witness the hanging, which took place in between the White Plains courthouse and prison. Only those with a pass were permitted to attend.

During the weeks leading up to the hanging, rumors intensified that an assault would take place at the gallows to free Isaac from his doom. The court responded by erecting a high board fence enclosing the grounds' perimeter and intensifying security by adding a regiment of the National Guard. All available deputy sheriffs and peace officers from throughout the county were called upon and ready to repel the expected assault.

The hanging of Isaac Van Wart Buckhout would be Westchester's first execution since 1856 and the fifth since the American Revolution. The gallows, consisting of a cross beam and a drop weight of 398 pounds, were freshly made and would be used for the first time. Many people traveled a great distance in hopes of witnessing the execution. Two people from Sleepy Hollow even offered $50 for two passes.

Shortly after 11 am on February 16, Isaac Buckhout briefly conversed with his only surviving sibling, Benjamin, who wept as Isaac hugged him for the last time. "Ike, we will not be long separated."

Meanwhile, the crowd grew around the gallows. Nine Third Regiment National Guard companies were there to keep things organized. They had a. They arrived earlier in the morning and fortified themselves with whisky. Several of them climbed on top of the courthouse, while another cluster began whooping and yelling while beating drums, to the great annoyance of the sheriff.

Isaac then marched directly to the platform as the clergy read. Isaac shook the sheriff's hand, then turned to a reporter and said, "I hope, my friend, when I am gone, that you will tell the public that Sheriff Brundage has made me very comfortable."

Isaac's blue eyes stared at the large crowd, smiling and nodding as he walked unassisted down the stone steps, looking more like a man about to get married than one marching to his execution. He wore a white shirt with no collar, under a black vest, and with a gray fleck coat and gray pantaloons. He carelessly glanced at the gallows as he stepped on the ground before walking directly under the hangman's noose.

A reverend gave a short prayer, followed by Sheriff Robert Brundage asking if the 39-year-old convicted murderer had any last words. "No. All I have to say is - goodbye. God bless you."

The executioner covered Isaac's large round head with a black cap. He tied Isaac's legs together and then tightened the rope around Isaac's neck and fastened it to the one hanging above the murderer's head. A few moments later, at 11:42 am, the crowd heard the dull thud of an ax.

The weight fell, causing Isaac's 200-pound body to jerk up about three feet. He clenched his fists tightly as the rope settled into its place. After a minute or so, his chest heaved several times, followed by violent trembles. After four minutes of hanging still, he drew his legs up three times, after which they fell limp and motionless.

Dr. Hodgeson, the jail physician, took Isaac's pulse, which ceased to beat after nine minutes. After 14 minutes, the doctor pronounced him dead, at which point he ordered Isaac's body lowered.

At 12:02 pm, a Coroner's jury viewed the body and removed the rope from his neck and the black cap from his face. They placed Isaac in a silver-mounted rosewood coffin lined with white satin. The post-mortem examination determined he died from strangulation and that the hanging did not cause Isaac's neck to break.

The site of the gallows is now White Plains Masonic Lodge #473 on Martine Avenue.

Sheriff Brundage turned Isaac's body over to his brother Benjamin. Reports said Benjamin had Isaac buried in Chappaqua, NY, beside his parents, though they didn't provide specific details.

It's believed that Benjamin buried Isaac in an unmarked grave at the Friends Cemetery on 420 Quaker Road in Chappaqua. Francis Spies' *Book of Deaths* extracted from "Chappaqua, NY Quaker Records" lists the cemetery's burials, which include #242 Anna Louisa Coop Buckhout and #243 Isaac Van Wart Buckhout. It's unclear if she's buried near her murderer.

A few weeks later, on March 14, 1872, the *Port Chester Journal* published:

*"The feeling obtains and daily strengthens that Buckhout is still living and is now out of the country. This idea seems to originate in the fact that the neck of the unfortunate man was not broken by the act of execution - many people believe that dislocation was prepared against - that he was not taken to Chappaqua and buried, but that his body was secretly conveyed to some private place and suspended animation restored by means of electricity."*

A few years later, the Buckhout house burned down. Shortly after that, Ira Miller, the man Isaac Buckhout confessed to, was in court, accused of selling a 12-acre property and a pair of oxen to a woman for $35,000 without having a deed. The judge for the case was Judge Barnard, the same man who had sent Isaac Buckhout to the gallows.

In 1890, Ezra Yerks, who worked at the Buckhout farm with his brother Isaac and his wife Elizabeth at the time of the 1869 murders, passed away. After Ezra's death, his brother searched his belongings and found a box containing gold, silver, and paper money at least 30 years old. The box's contents are worth about $200,000 by today's standards. It is unclear how he acquired it.

# 5.) HULDA THE WITCH

Within the same cemetery where Isaac Van Wart Buckhout's murder victim Alfred Rendall and his son Charles are buried, is an eerie grave with an epitaph that immediately stands out. This particular headstone at the Sleepy Hollow Cemetery reads:

*Hulda of Bohemia. Died 1777. Herbalist, Healer. Patriot. Felled by the British while protecting the Militia.*

Locals know her by her more famous name, Hulda the Witch.

Author Edgar Mayew Bacon may have been the first to write about Hulda. His 1897 book, *Chronicles of Tarrytown and Sleepy Hollow*, dedicates several pages to her. However, it remains open to debate whether he based his writing on facts, fiction, or somewhere in between.

Mr. Bacon describes Hulda as a mysterious woman who lived in a small cottage on the outskirts of town, in the woods, near Spook Rock, during the American Revolution.

The large boulder in the woods has been the setting for numerous urban legends retold for generations. Among them is that Native American hunters witnessed the ghosts of dancing women on top of the rock. Washington Irving even mentions the mysterious rock in "The Legend of Sleepy Hollow." He also mentions the place being bewitched by a high German doctor, whom some believe could be Hulda.

It's unclear whether Hulda may have emigrated from Germany or if there's any truth to the rumor a Native American sachem raised her, which is how she was able to communicate and trade hand-woven baskets with local Weckquaesgeeks.

Mr. Bacon wrote that Hulda enjoyed gathering herbs from the forest for home remedies. Her cottage was full of the distinct odor of drying plants, which may have led to rumors of her witch-like powers spreading among the valley's inhabitants, causing them to fear her.

When the Revolutionary War began, Hulda desired to join a local militia to defend her home. However, they refused her admittance. As the Revolution progressed and The Redcoats began marching closer to Tarrytown, Hulda took matters and a musket into her own hands. It's written that she died heroically in a shootout with British soldiers near Spook Rock, defending the land of locals who shunned her.

After Hulda's death, the villagers brought her body back to her hut. Surprisingly, they found a Bible with a note inside. Hulda had willed her gold to the American Revolution widows and written this in rudimentary Dutch. To make up for the way they had treated her, the community gave her a Christian burial. However, they still considered her a witch and buried her in an unmarked grave in an isolated area of the Old Dutch Burying Ground.

It is uncertain whether Hulda was an actual historical figure in Sleepy Hollow during the Revolutionary War or a work of fiction created by the imagination of an 1800s author. However, in August 2019, a gravestone bearing the enigmatic name Hulda of Bohemia was discovered in Sleepy Hollow Cemetery.

 Shortly after, a practicing witch from Ossining named Carla Hall, who enjoys local history and previously worked at the Old Dutch Church's recurring "Legend of Sleepy Hollow" event, developed a production based on Hulda. Titled "Hulda, The Other Legend of Sleepy Hollow," it's told from the perspective of Abby, an African American girl based on Hall's research into enslaved people who lived at Philipsburg Manor. In Hall's story, Abby meets Hulda at a time when both of these women were forced to live on the edges of society.

 For possible upcoming dates to see "Hulda, The Other Legend of Sleepy Hollow," please refer to the Old Dutch Church's website:

www.VisitSleepyHollow.com/old-dutch-church

# 6.) THE PIRATE?

The concept of a legendary pirate's ghost guarding a buried treasure may seem like a plot from an episode of the animated series *Scooby Doo Where Are You?*, but it's also been an urban legend associated with Sleepy Hollow for generations.

Author Edgar Mayhew Bacon, who wrote about Hulda the Witch, also wrote about Captain Kidd's Rock:

*"This has long been the name of a rock that is part of the river wall on the outer side of Kingsland's Point. There is a summer house built over the rock, and if there were ever golden riches beneath it, or if there are still treasures, it is not (fortunately) the duty of a sober historian to tell."*

The tale references a large boulder at the edge of Sleepy Hollow's Kingsland Point waterfront park on the Hudson River. According to lore, the legendary pirate captain held covert meetings with Tarrytown manor owner Frederick Philipse at this location.

The word "pirate" perhaps conjures up images of a cartoon Captain Hook or Johnny Depp as Captain Jack Sparrow in the *Pirates of The Caribbean* films. It may also create the urge to mutter sounds like "Arrr!" or phrases like "yo-ho-ho matey!" It's unsurprising, as fictional books and movies created most of what we think we know about how pirates acted and talked.

The fictional antagonist of Robert Louis Stevenson's 1883 novel *Treasure Island* has dramatically influenced the modern iconography of the pirate and arguably the most well-known fictional pirate ever. The colorful outfits, pirate hat, and talking parrot sidekick were all things that originated with this character. In Disney's 1950 film adaption, actor Robert Newton portrayed Long John Silver and introduced new aspects to the character, most notably pirate lingo.

Robert Newtown originated the now-stereotypical pirate accent, which movies and television have duplicated since his portrayal as Silver. His improvisational creations include phrases like "landlubber" and the iconic "Arrr!"

The motion picture Long John Silver character became so popular that in 1969, it became the namesake for a fast-food seafood chain. Today, more than 1,100 Long John Silver locations are across 41 states. As Newton's portrayal of Long John Silver grew in popularity, the lines between historical pirates from the Golden Age of Piracy in the 17th and early 18th centuries and fictional movie pirates began to blur.

Beyond the jargon and talking parrot sidekicks, the idea of pirates burying treasure chests is another aspect typically associated with pirate life. However, there is only a historical record of one pirate burying a treasure, Captain William Kidd.

Next to only perhaps Blackbeard, Captain Kidd is arguably the most well-known historical pirate. While his life was full of adventure, danger, and mystery, a surprising twist is that he consistently denied being a pirate.

Born in Scotland in 1654, William Kidd's first gig was in England, where he was hired as a young sailor to capture pirates and foreign vessels, causing a threat to his country.

In 1691, Kidd relocated to New York City. He married a wealthy widow named Sarah, lived with her at 119 Pearl Street, and owned property on Wall Street. At the time, England and France were at war with each other. Sailing was dangerous as ambushes from pirates were common.

New York's governor, Lord Bellomont, suggested Kidd be given a privateering contract that would allow him to attack enemy vessels, including French and pirate ships. Privateers could attack and raid ships legally, whereas pirates did so without the proper government paperwork.

According to local lore, while living in New York City, Captain Kidd befriended Frederick Philipse. Philipse would light a fire on the now-famous boulder bearing Kidd's name to signal for him to come ashore to discuss business.

Philipse came to America from The Netherlands and, like Kidd, married a wealthy widow. He ended up owning a 52,000-acre manor on the Hudson. It's believed he amassed his fortune in trade with pirates, including the buying, trading, and selling of enslaved people.

While it's unclear what may have transpired between Captain Kidd and Frederick Philipse, historians have identified at least 115 named individuals enslaved by the Philipse family at their properties in Manhattan and Sleepy Hollow.

Soon after, Governor Bellomont set Kidd up with the massive 34-gun *Adventure Galley*. With his new vessel, Kidd set sail for Madagascar in the Indian Ocean, a hotbed for pirate activity. However, he found no pirate or French vessels to seize, and about a third of his crew had died from the disease.

In August 1697, Kidd attacked a convoy of Indian treasure ships, but a much larger East India Company warship drove him off. This attack violated Kidd's charter, and the lines between privateer and pirate began to blur.

Things escalated a year later, in January 1698, when Kidd captured the *Queddah Merchant*, a treasure ship heading home from the Far East. It was a Moorish ship with cargo owned by Armenians. The vessel allegedly sailed with French papers, so Kidd used that to justify selling off the cargo. The haul was about 15,000 British pounds (over two million dollars in modern times).

Soon after, Kidd ran into a pirate ship captained by notorious English pirate Robert Culliford. The two had first met in 1689 as shipmates aboard the French privateer *The Sainte Rose* before going their separate ways. Allegedly, the old pals greeted each other warmly and traded supplies and news. Unfortunately, as Kidd embraced a well-known English pirate, many of his men deserted him at this point, running off with their share of the treasure.

Meanwhile, news of Kidd turning pirate reached England. Kidd's backers quickly wanted nothing to do with him. Upon reaching the

Caribbean, Kidd learned he was denounced as a pirate and had several men of war searching for him.

 To avoid recognition, he ditched his famed ship in favor of a new small boat. Before returning to the United States, Kidd buried part of his treasure on Gardiner's Island, off the coast of Long Island, NY, hoping to use the valuables as a future bargaining chip.

 Aware of the accusations against Kidd, New York governor Lord Bellomont, who was away in Massachusetts, lured Kidd to meet him in Boston. Kidd agreed as he felt he had an ally in the governor who had previously endorsed him. However, despite their previous friendship and Kidd's belief in innocence, Lord Bellmont's own fear of being implicated in piracy led him to turn against Kidd.

 Lord Bellomont had Kidd arrested on July 6, 1699, and placed in Boston's Stone Prison, where he spent most of the time in solitary confinement. Some believe the harsh prison conditions led to a decline in Kidd's mental health. His wife, Sarah, was also arrested and imprisoned. They never saw each other again.

 Kidd spent two years in prison, during which time Lord Bellomeont reportedly found Kidd's buried treasure on Gardiner's Island and planned to use it as evidence against him during his upcoming trial in England.

 Meanwhile, Frederick Philipse allegedly continued to trade guns, alcohol, and other supplies in demand by pirates for enslaved people. In 1698, after eight years of service on the governor's executive council,

Lord Bellomont banned Philipse from government office for conducting slave trading in New York.

Kidd's trial took place on May 8, 1701. The 47-year-old Kidd pleaded that he had never turned pirate but was found guilty. He was hanged on May 23, 1701, and his body was put into an iron cage hanging along the River Thames, which served as a warning to other pirates.

Treasure hunters remain convinced that Kidd buried additional treasure before his execution. Some believe the area of Kidd's Rock in Sleepy Hollow is a possible location for the buried loot. Others proclaim that Huckleberry Island off the coast of nearby New Rochelle is the rightful location.

Both of those spots, along with Liberty Island near the pedestal of the Statue of Liberty, are rumored to be routinely guarded by Captain Kidd's ghost.

In 1930, after being nudged by persuasive treasure hunters, the Parks Commission shoveled away at "Money Hill" at Croton Point Park in the Westchester town of Croton. They failed to recover any pirate treasure.

The legend of Captain Kidd's buried treasure has been the subject of countless books, movies, and television shows. It has become the basis of pirate treasure hunts, capturing the public's imagination for centuries after the execution of the notorious captain, who may not have actually been a pirate.

Frederick Philipse died in 1702 and is buried with his two wives in the crypt of the Old Dutch Church in Sleepy Hollow.

Philipse's property was passed to his son, Frederick Philipse II, and eventually to his grandson, Frederick Philipse III.

A few years into the Revolution, Frederick Philipse III and his family, who were Loyalists, were arrested for treason. The manor was confiscated in 1779 and used as collateral to raise funds for the Colonial cause.

After the war, it was sold at a public auction, split between 287 buyers. The lower parcel went to Cornelius Low before eventually being passed to numerous owners until 1951, when it was acquired by Sleepy Hollow Restorations, now known as Historic Hudson Valley.

Local philanthropist John D. Rockefeller Jr. funded the restoration of about 20 acres, which became today's Philipsburgh Manor historic site. On November 5, 1961, it became designated as a National Historic Landmark, joined the National Register of Historic Places in 1966, and is now open as a museum at 381 North Broadway in Sleepy Hollow.

In 1978, a worker at the 300-year-old estate reported seeing a figure standing on the stairs outside a bedroom. It was later determined that one could have been there. Centuries earlier, in 1740, 10-year-old manor resident Mary Philispe described seeing a mysterious cloaked figure leading her into a tunnel under the house.

# 7.) UNDERGROUND RAILROAD

Westchester County, a pivotal location in the Underground Railroad, was a beacon of hope for enslaved African Americans seeking freedom from the South to the North and Canada. Despite its illegality, numerous individuals displayed immense courage, risking their lives to aid these escapees. The county's role in this network of secret routes and safe houses is a testament to such bravery.

As Underground Railroad activity was secretive in the 1860s, detailed information about its operations remains hidden as their movements were undocumented. Historians believe Westchester had two underground railroad routes crossing through the county. White Quakers who opposed slavery risked their lives running a route scattered throughout Westchester, which included rumored safe houses and stations at the home of John Carpenter in Scarsdale and the Stony Hill section of Buckout Road on the border of eastern White Plains and western Harrison.

Moses Pierce, a Quaker with a heart for justice, is said to have aided Underground Railroad leader Harriet Tubman in her mission to smuggle numerous enslaved people to freedom. His house, a sanctuary of hope, served as the second stop on a route from New York City to the John Jay Homestead in Bedford and ultimately to freedom in Canada.

The second of Westchester's Underground Railroad routes followed the eastern shore of the Hudson River, up from New York City by train or by foot through Hastings-on-Hudson, Dobbs Ferry, and Tarrytown to Montreal, Quebec. According to local folklore, the Tarrytown home of an Underground Railroad conductor named Amanda Foster was among the stops.

Born in Albany in 1807 to a servant in New York Governor DeWitt Clinton's household, Amanda was taken from her enslaved mother when she was just six weeks old. Her life took her on a journey, sailing up and down the Hudson as a waitress on a riverboat in her teens. This journey eventually led her to become a significant figure in the Underground Railroad.

Amanda married a man named John Bowman and later worked as a nurse for the governor of Arkansas. After receiving the papers that declared her a free woman, she sailed south, loaning her papers to an enslaved girl in Louisville, KY.

After settling in Tarrytown, her husband opened a barbershop, and Amanda had a candy and ice cream store located at 124 Main Street. However, when John died two years later, Amanda returned to work on the Hudson River, this time as a barber aboard the steamship *Washington Irving*.

In 1845, she returned to Tarrytown and opened another candy store. She also got married to a barber named Henry Foster. After twenty years, Amanda and her new husband, who had formerly been enslaved, founded the Foster Memorial AME Zion Church at Wildey Avenue in Tarrytown.

For five years before its completion in 1864, the congregation met in Amanda's candy store. According to local historians, visitors to the church included Underground Railroad conductor Harriet Tubman.

The church is now the oldest continuously used African American church in Westchester County and stands next to the house where Amanda lived, where she sheltered runaway slaves fleeing for freedom.

A few years after Amanda passed away in 1904, a remarkable Black woman born to formerly enslaved parents lived a few miles away. Sarah Breedlove was born in Delta, Louisiana, in 1867, the first of her siblings born into freedom after the 1863 signing of the Emancipation Proclamation.

Orphaned at seven, married by 14, and a widowed mother by 18, Sarah began to lose her hair a few years later from a scalp condition.

She responded by experimenting with various hair care products in the early 1900s, eventually creating an original formula. She branded it "Madam Walker's Wonderful Hair Grower" and assumed the new identity of Madam C.J. Walker.

Her product became a huge success, leading to her creating a hair care product line specifically for African American women. Madam Walker was a shrewd entrepreneur who leveraged her marketing skills to promote her line of hair care products. She traveled extensively around the United States, delivering demonstrations and lectures on hair care.

Additionally, she established a beauty school to train women to use her products and start their own businesses. To provide African American women with opportunities for financial independence, Madam Walker employed them as "beauty culturists" to sell her hair care products.

As her business grew, Walker became one of the country's wealthiest self-made women. In 1918, she purchased a 32-room mansion in Irvington. Located less than three miles from the Foster Memorial AME Zion Church, Walker's mansion on 67 North Broadway was designed by the first licensed African American architect, Vertner Tandy.

Madam Walker used her wealth to support various philanthropic causes, including education and the arts. She donated to the Tuskegee Institute and The National Association for the Advancement of Colored People and established scholarships for African American students. Her mansion, which she called Villa Lewaro, became a symbol of Walker's success and a gathering place for African American intellectuals and artists. The home overlooking the Hudson River cost $600,000 in 1912 (about twenty million dollars today) and featured many lavish furnishings, including a 24-karat gold piano.

Madam Walker passed away in 1919, but the legacy of a remarkable entrepreneur and philanthropist, born to formerly enslaved people who became the first African American millionaire, lives on.

Madam Walker left her estate to her daughter, A'Leila Walker. After she died in 1931, Villa Lewaro was left to the NAACP.

# 8.) BUTTERMILK HILL

"Buttermilk Hill" is the name of a rugged and desolate mountain about two miles away from Swan Lake in Tarrytown. The journey to reach its peak is not for the faint-hearted but for those ready to face nature's raw power. The path is lined with dense growth of young trees, rocks, and underbrush that are a testament to the untamed beauty of nature. To reach the top of the mountain, you must navigate a lonesome, tortuous, rocky wood road that starts from the Sawmill River Road at the foot of the hill on its eastern side. The distance from the base to the top of the mountain is about half a mile, a challenge that only the most determined would undertake.

When European settlers first explored the mountain, they discovered multiple varieties of trees and an abundance of wild animals, including bears, wolves, possums, badgers, weasels, and numerous bird species. At its highest point, about 711 feet above the water of the Long Island Sound, Buttermilk Hill is the second tallest in Westchester County.

The origin story of Buttermilk Hill's name is a fascinating tale of determination and perseverance. It shows how the local farmers overcame the challenges posed by the American Revolution and protected their valuable dairy cows from theft. The farmers' wives played a crucial role in this endeavor by hiding the cattle in the ravines of the long hill, making butter beside the little woodland waterfalls, and carrying milk, cream, and butter down the hillsides at night to avoid Cowboys. The legend of the farmer's wife who spilled her milk pail and inadvertently gave Buttermilk Hill its name is a testament to the enduring power of storytelling and community spirit.

On a detached portion of the steep, rocky eastern side of Buttermilk Hill is the allegedly haunted Raven Rock. Numerous urban legends are associated with it, including one about a woman who strayed from a nearby trail during a snowstorm and sought shelter from the chilling wind in the ravine behind the spooky boulder. Unfortunately, the snow drifted in on her, and she fell asleep, never to wake up again.

Since then, the ravine has been considered a sad and lonely refuge. According to the legend, the spirit of the deceased woman haunts the ravine, appearing at times as a ghostly apparition to lost wanderers, urging them to stay away from the ravine that proved fatal for her.

Eerily, other ghosts, including the spirits of a Native American girl killed by a jealous lover and a Revolutionary War-era girl who fled from the dreadful attentions of an amorous Loyalist raider, are also linked to Raven Rock, albeit with little details.

There's also a version that incorporates all of these ghost stories, stating that a Native American girl was set to elope with a British officer, and while waiting for him to arrive at Raven Rock, she froze to death.

Washington Irving even references Raven Rock in "The Legend of Sleepy Hollow" when elder villagers tell Ichabod Crane local ghost stories.

*"Some mention was also made of the woman in white, that haunted the dark glen at Raven Rock and was often heard to shriek on winter nights before a storm, having perished there in the snow."*

While it remains unclear if a ghostly woman dressed in white haunts Raven Rock during snowstorms, during the 1800s, Buttermilk Hill became the site of tragedy and violent murders.

There's minimal documentation about the mother of Leander Hammond. According to an 1881 article in the *Eastern State Journal*, an unknown person murdered her at the foot of Buttermilk Hill in the 1860s. The newspaper also reported that a drover was killed and thrown into a nearby well a few years prior. The newspaper only referenced these tragic events when Clinton Hammond, Leander's son, was called to testify in the case of The Buttermilk Hill Ax Murderer.

The crime occurred at the end of August 1881 in an open field near Patrick Coleman's farm property on top of Buttermilk Hill's peak. The 65-year-old farmer told the police an unknown assailant killed his helper, 35-year-old Joseph Baldwin.

*"I saw a negro man, a negro boy, attack the murdered man with clubs and flee to the woods."*

Coroner Schirmer arrived at the scene a few hours later as Joseph Baldwin's body continued to lay in the blazing sun. His initial examination of the corpse revealed that Coleman had lied to the police because the man's death was caused by the blows of an ax.

Baldwin received a blow with the back of an ax on the left side of his head, which split his ear entirely in two and broke his jaw. The mark of the pole of the ax was distinctly definite. There was another wound on the left side of the forehead, which crushed the skull, made with the corner of the ax. On top of the head was a cut about four inches long, made with the ax's blade, severing the skull and causing his brain to protrude.

In addition to this damming evidence, a few feet from Baldwin's body, Coroner Schirmer found a bloody ax with a broken handle, which Coleman admitted to owning.

Mr. Coleman's murder trial started that September. He maintained his innocence stating,

*"A little negro had been nutting, Baldwin was working, and he tried to take the bag of nuts away from him. They had a tussle, and a big negro came out of the bushes and struck Baldwin with clubs."*

After a brief consultation, the jury returned. Two charged Coleman with criminal responsibility, and seven found him guilty of murder. Late that October, Mr. Coleman, the accused ax murderer of Buttermilk Hill, posted bail of $2,500 and was released from jail.

What became of Mr. Coleman or his farm after the incident is unclear. A few years later, however, in August 1902, Buttermilk Hill was purchased by John D. Rockefeller and added to the already massive estate of America's wealthiest man.

A year later, in 1903, Mr. Rockefeller and his son placed traps around their property after multiple local sightings of a loose panther. It's unknown where the panther came from, but it's believed to have made its home on Buttermilk Hill and is responsible for missing chickens and sheep from several local farms.

A week or so later, a thrilling hunting party embarked on a nocturnal adventure, stalking the panther across Rockefeller's vast 5,000-acre estate. The hunters, their hearts pounding, reported they had tracked the beast, fired five shots at it, and believed they had killed it.

Yet, to everyone's surprise, the report lacked concrete evidence, and panther sightings persisted. Credible witnesses continued to describe seeing a five-foot-long animal with dark brown fur, adding to the mystery.

The hunters returned and followed strange footprints in the snow until the panther appeared and ferociously launched at its unsuspecting attackers. Guns fired, and panther blood covered the snow of Buttermilk Hill.

With the panther exterminated, Mr. Rockefeller offered a bounty for killing other animals on his estate. In 1906, he offered to pay 25 cents for all snakes killed on his estate. As the property had an abundance of blacksnakes, garter snakes, and copperheads, an abundance of local boys began snake hunting. Mr. Rockefeller also offered $2 for the killing of every dog on his property, which led to some trouble with his neighbors.

In June 1927, two local schoolboys hiking on Buttermilk Hill discovered a fleshless skeleton. Edward and Ray Peters found the human remains lying in the woods on the rocky slope of the hill on an isolated part of Rockefeller's estate. The skeleton had one leg tucked under its torso and the other wedged against a tree. The person's clothes were tattered and rotted away.

The police investigated and, despite finding a crack in the skull, ruled out murder. Their examination determined the middle-aged man may have been dead for nearly two years. They believe he may have been descending the steep slope of the hill, slipped, and fractured his head.

On June 3, 1935, a watchman at the Rockefeller estate made a gruesome discovery. While making his daily rounds around Buttermilk Hill, he found the corpse of a man hanging from a tree. The police identified the man as 50-year-old Stephen Cipely, who emigrated from Poland in 1905 and has resided for the past few years at a nearby retirement home. The police could not determine a motive.

# 9.) SEVEN UNSOLVED MURDERS

Over a century ago, seven mysterious and gruesome murders in the neighborhood rocked the local community.

### I. 1875 - The Night Watchman

On a chilling January 8, 1875, a violent event unfolded at the country home of St. Louis, Kansas City, and Northern Missouri Railroad Company president William Hoge. Nestled a mere mile from Washington Irving's former residence, Sunnyside, William Hoge's country estate had been closed for several months. During this time, Mr. Hoge entrusted the property to a 28-year-old Canadian servant named William McMullen, who was to act as its watchman.

Shortly after 8 pm on January 8, McMullen suddenly entered the nearby home of Mr. Hoge's brother-in-law, Captain Herring, about a quarter-mile up the road. Wildy crying from physical pain, McMullen frighteningly conveyed to Captain Herring that a burglar had shot him.

A physician rushed to the scene and discovered a bullet entered the right side of McMullen's abdomen, near his groin, and after passing through the body, had emerged from the back near the hip bone. Two additional surgical doctors arrived shortly after. However, a day later, Mr. McMullen died.

As news of the event spread, neighborhood residents became puzzled. Their surprise focused on why none of the doctors who attended to the dying man made the case known to authorities.

Before Mr. McMullen died, he said that a little before 8 pm, he lit a candle in the room where he slept and then heard a noise as though people were walking on the piazza above him. When he investigated, he found a tall man standing up against the house, close to the door. At the same time, McMullen spotted a shorter man on the porch. As McMullen approached the men to see if he recognized them, the shorter man shot him.

With this news, Constable Lawrence investigated the crime scene. He found that a bullet had embedded itself in a column supporting the room of the veranda. Upon further investigation, he found the tracks of two people in the snow going in a contrary direction from the house. This discovery led Lawrence to believe that after McMullen fled for his life with a bullet wound, the two burglars rapidly left the scene, taking lengthy strides.

One set of tracks led directly down the hill toward the railroad station, while the other continued in a southerly direction and eventually lost sight of it in a ravine. A month later, Governor Tilden offered a $500 reward for the apprehension of McMullen's murderer. No arrests have been made in this century-plus-old case.

<u>II - The Heroic Storekeeper</u>

Violence at Tarrytown shops and stores increased during the late 1800s. In 1883, a masked woman entered a local barber shop and fired two shots, striking barber John McCarthy, who, fortunately, survived the assault but had no idea who the shooter was.

On February 20, 1899, while trying to prevent a shooting in his Tarrytown grocery store, 35-year-old John Ledwith took a fatal bullet through the heart. Ledwith was survived by a wife and a young child. The police began a manhunt for the murder suspect.

After weeks of searching, Charles Nossiter, the chief of the Tarrytown police, arrested a 26-year-old Black man named Harrison Howard for killing Ledwith, whom he found in Kingston. After arresting him, Nossiter took him to the White Plains jail and collected a $500 reward from Westchester County and a $100 reward from The Emmet Club of Tarrytown, where Mr. Lediwith was president.

*The Yonkers Herald* printed,

*"The place where Ledwith was shot has been the scene of several other tragedies. At least half a dozen men have died there through violence, and several years ago, a man named Buschel was murdered there."*

That May, Harrison Howard took the stand at his murder trial. He testified that he only fired the gun in self-defense after he had been beaten and stabbed by one of the crowd in Ledwith's store. His clothing was put into evidence to show multiple cuts, and he displayed a visible knife scar on his back. Perhaps his convincing testimony is what led to the jury not finding him guilty of murder, saving him from death by the electric chair. Instead, they found him guilty of manslaughter in the first degree. Justice Hierschberg sentenced Howard to serve ten years and ten months in State Prison.

 Howard's trial caused a rise in racial tensions, which escalated even more after a Black man named Charles Lester brutally assaulted a 6-year-old girl as she returned home from school. The girl's father, Michael Connellan, reported that Lester seized her as she walked home through a dense part of the woods. Mr. Connellan heard his daughter's screams and ran to her, armed with a loaded revolver. He found his daughter unconscious as her assailant fled, only to be apprehended a short while later by the police. He was sentenced to a prison term of 16 years.

 Only a week later, the police arrested Tarrytown fruit store owner Joe Couti for assaulting a 12-year-old girl. According to her story, the Italian store owner grabbed her by the arm, dragged her into a back room, and then threw her on a sofa. An employee walked in, breaking up the incident, but was assaulted by Couti. Afterward, another woman, Eva Delaney, came forward and told the police that six months prior, an unknown man bound her to the same sofa in Couti's Tarrytown fruit store and assaulted her.

### III - Stabbed In The Back

In January 1903, someone murdered Samuel Wisner in North Tarrytown by stabbing him in his back. The police found Wisner in the doorway of Goldman's furniture store on Courtland Street, a few blocks from his Clinton Street home.

Their theory is that Wisner got into a fight at a nearby Italian saloon, was stabbed with a stiletto knife, and then thrown against the furniture store's heavy plate-glass door to make it appear he had drunkenly fallen against the glass and cut himself.

Wisner did not regain consciousness after the police found him. The stab wound, which went through the victim's spine, caused him to die on the way to the hospital. The police theorized he may have learned some of the inner doings of an Italian secret society and was stabbed to prevent him from revealing them to the police. No arrests were made.

### IV - A Suspicious Death

The 1903 death certificate written for 65-year-old Ezekiel Bevier stated his cause of death was paralysis. But it wasn't until two weeks after his burial that his sister, Mrs. A.H. Pardee, and his nephew, J.C. Pardee, were notified of his passing.

J.C. Pardee believed someone killed his uncle during a robbery and asked the Tarrytown police to investigate Uncle Ezekiel's death as a murder, even offering a $2,000 reward for the arrest and conviction of his uncle's slayer.

Someone who attended Ezekiel's funeral told J.C. that he noticed discolorations and bruises on the dead man's face. Not waiting for the police, J.C. Pardee went to his uncle's neighborhood and gathered information.

He learned that a few weeks prior, a boy passing Ezekiel's farm was attracted to him frantically tapping on the window and motioning for him to come in. When the boy entered, he found the room in disorder and Ezekiel unconscious on the floor. The exertion of getting to the window exhausted him, and he had wounds on his head and face.

J.C. Pardee also learned that when the boy notified doctors, a Pleasantville doctor, Dr. Wilcox, determined Ezekiel's wounds were consistent with being hit in the face with a sandbag and bodily bruises consistent with being kicked with a boot heel.

Two days after this, a new doctor, Dr. Mills, relieved Dr. Wilcox and ordered Ezekiel removed to a private hospital in Tarrytown.

Mr. Pardee said that although his uncle's head was crushed and his body covered with wounds, nobody reported the case to the police, and nobody notified the victim's relatives of what happened until two weeks after the body had been buried.

## V - CASINO KILLING

Built in 1895, the Ardsley Casino, located near the Ardsley-on-Hudson train station and the New York Yacht Club dock on the eastern bank of the Hudson River, became a playground for the rich and famous of New York society. The casino was established by 19th-century luminaries, including John D. Rockefeller, J.P. Morgan, and Cornelius Vanderbilt II.

The grounds included a golf course, six grass and clay tennis courts, an indoor swimming pool, horse stables, a baseball diamond, and a polo ground. In May 1903, the Tarrytown police were on the premises to investigate a murder.

Someone fatally shot John Heffernan, a coachman, on a little private sidewalk around 8:30 pm on Sunday, May 24, in Tarrytown, shortly after he left the casino with his girlfriend Sarah Campbell. Numerous patrons at the casino saw Heffernan before he died and told their varying stories to Tarrytown's Chief Abercrombie, implicating multiple prominent members of the neighborhood.

As the police sorted out conflicting witness accounts, rumors spread around town that the murder was actually a case of mistaken identity. The local belief became that the shooter mistook Heffernan and his girlfriend for other people, though it's unknown who or why.

Another baseless theory, advanced by Heffernan's employer, Max E. Sand, is that Heffernan and his girlfriend accidentally surprised the gunman, who became frightened and opened fire, fearing he was about to be held up.

The murder mystery continued for several weeks until a break in the case happened in early June.

A woman phoned the Tarrytown police after two tramps resembling the descriptions of men wanted in connection with the murder appeared at her front door. However, the two men, going door to door selling court plaster, were never arrested.

Instead, after Sarah Campbell and a 15-year-old witness came forward with additional recounts of the night in question, the police searched for a man described by witnesses as a "tall, well-built fellow with a light, stubby mustache, light hair, and hatless." No arrests have been made in the case.

## VI - Taxi Driver

At an early hour on Tuesday, September 6, 1904, the body of a North Tarrytown taxi driver was found in a wagon in an outlying stable with multiple stab wounds. The police identified the victim as 24-year-old George Daley. They were familiar with him as he had spent several terms in jail and was recently released from the Kings County Penitentiary.

For months before Daley's murder, he had numerous quarrels with several young men in town, leading up to Daley assaulting one of them.

On the night of the murder, Daley drove to a beer garden on Court Street until midnight and then went to Helfrich's Road House. The police learned that after Helfrich's, Daley insulted a pretty barmaid named Bedelia at the Pocantico Hotel. Whatever he said is unknown, but it caught the attention of two patrons, Morris Hartnett and William Kilday, an ex-police sergeant.

Kilday told police that after he separated Mr. Hartnett and Mr. Daley, Daley also allegedly got into an altercation with a man named Lynch, known locally as "The Man From Clamtown." Afterwards, Daley left the scene.

That was the last time Mr. Daley was seen alive. Shortly before dawn, his carriage, with no one driving, was seen in front of Farrington's Drug Store on Beekman Avenue in North Tarrytown, at which point someone led the deserted horse to the police station. There, officers discovered that Daley's murdered body lay in the rear of the vehicle, wedged down behind the seat by the murderers.

The police arrested William Kilday and Morris Hartnett as suspects; however, they allowed them to go free after spending about a month in jail.

The police found Daley with six stab wounds, any of which would have been fatal, and additional wounds on his body, legs, and head. Because of the numerous stab wounds on Daley's body, which look as though created by the use of an Italian stiletto knife, authorities theorized that Daley may have been a victim of Italian "Black Hand" gangsters, who took for an Italian who had failed to pay tribute to the society. Over the past two months before Daley's murder, Black Hand agents allegedly stabbed more than half a dozen Italians when they refused to pay money to the society.

## VII – THE BLONDE IN THE POND

In early June 1905, the police responded to a call in Tarrytown regarding the discovery of a body. The unknown deceased woman had been found in a pond on the estate of F.F. Lewis, a New York millionaire.

After the coroner removed the body to the morgue, the police received word that a 26-year-old Swedish woman named Hilda Johnson had been missing from her home in White Plains since Memorial Day. The body of the blonde woman found in the pond was 5'3' and 130 pounds, approximately the same as Hilda.

Reverend Anderson, who preaches every Sunday at Hilda's church, went to the morgue to identify the body. However, because it had so badly decomposed after being submerged in water for an estimated ten days, he failed to make an identification.

The police believe foul play was involved as the victim had a bump over her right eye, likely caused by a blow from a blunt object. No arrests were made.

# 10.) THE HERMIT

While numerous people, places, and events from the area may have inspired parts of Washington Irving's "The Legend of Sleepy Hollow," according to local lore, an eccentric villager may have inspired another of Irving's classic short stories from *The Sketchbook of Geoffrey Crayon.*

According to local oral history, Washington Irvington based characteristics of his character Rip Van Winkle on a late 1800s neighborhood hermit.

First published in 1819, Irving's iconic title character lives in a village at the foot of New York's Catskill Mountains in the years before the American Revolution. To avoid his wife's nagging, Rip Van Winkle goes squirrel hunting one day, meets some bearded men playing nine-pin bowling, and becomes so intoxicated that he falls asleep. He awakens 20 years later to find his wife has been dead for quite some time, and the world as he knew it has radically changed, including the deaths of many of his friends. The story became so popular that in 2002, the village of Irvington unveiled a life-size bronze statue of Irving's literary creation on Main Street.

While elements of the character are undoubtedly unique to Irving's imagination, many local historians believe a significant influence for Rip was a genuinely unconventional man named Johann Stolting.

Born in Germany, Johann arrived in Hastings, NY in 1835.   While perhaps an eccentric, Johann Wilhelm Stolting was well-educated and spoke multiple languages, including German, Greek, French, and Hebrew. While living in Westchester, he worked various jobs, such as a mailman, a teacher, and even a scientist. Despite his high education, job history, and being a landowner, he chose to become a recluse later in life.

Seen walking through Tarrytown in homemade clothing without shoes and locally selling buttons, he made himself on a homemade lathe; Johann became regionally known as "The Hermit of Irvington."

He lived in a small shed overlooking the Saw Mill River Valley and slept in a coffin he made of local chestnut wood. Generations ago, people recalled seeing Johann roaming the streets of the Hudson River villages and local woods, bathing in the Saw Mill and Hudson Rivers. He died in Irvington on January 10, 1888, buried in the same coffin he slept in.

Johann's grave is the only one marked in the village. His burial site is a few hundred feet west of the Saw Mill River Parkway, which was deliberately swerved in its vicinity to avoid disturbance.

# 11.) THE HUDSON RIVER

Eerie tales of Westchester's famous Hudson River may be traceable to Washington Irving's "Rip Van Winkle." The 1819 short story reveals that the bearded men who play nine-pin bowling with Rip are ghosts from Henry Hudson's ship, *The Half Moon.*

Edgar Mayhew Bacon's 1897 *The Chronicles of Tarrytown* tells a whimsical account of seeing a ghost the Hudson River, thought to be perhaps Hudson's *Half Moon* or infamous pirate ship *The Flying Dutchman.*

Whether or not there's a ghost ship stalking the Hudson, or if it's simply the product of a fictional tale remains debatable. In any event, sometimes the truth is stranger than fiction, which is perhaps the case in the following six tales involving the Hudson River.

## I. - THE SEA SERPENT

"Kipsy" became the nickname for a giant sea serpent reputed to live in the Hudson River near Poughkeepsie. First spotted in 1610, the alleged creature has been sighted numerous times since.

Some believers suggest that a small population of Zeuglodons, a prehistoric toothed whale thought to have gone extinct 34 million years ago, may persist in parts of the world.

*The New York Times* published several articles about Kipsy, including one in 1895 where a man named Philip Jackson from Newark, New Jersey, claimed to have seen a 100-foot-long serpent swimming through the water.

Some Putnam County, NY residents have recalled that 1989 they were made aware of a threat to house pets that went missing near the railroad tracks next to the Hudson River. That spring, bones of cats and dogs were found along the sandy beaches near the river. Some locals attributed this to the Hudson River Monster, rumored to reside near an island that houses the ruins of the old Bannerman's Castle.

## II – WHO WAS SHE

In June 1891, a man noticed the body of a woman floating in the Hudson River off Croton Landing. He pulled her and notified the police. After an investigation, the victim was identified as an actress named Dolly Davis and thought to be a suicide.

Things became confusing after Dolly Davis turned out to be alive and well. She was even interviewed  by reporters a few days after her falsely reported death.

Later that month, a man and a young girl visited the morgue in Tarrytown. After viewing the body, the man said, "That's my wife. I have found her."

He identified himself as a traveling salesman named Frank Atwood and confirmed the deceased woman was his wife, Purcell Marinia.

The police believed the case was closed until two women showed up at the morgue a few weeks later. They positively identified the mystery woman as Mary Eugenie Josephine Arigaesei, a seamstress for Edward M. Field.

Edward M. Field was the son of Cyrus West Field, a successful American businessman who, along with other entrepreneurs, created the Atlantic Telegraph Company and laid the first telegraph cable across the Atlantic Ocean in 1858.

Cyrus Field was so powerful that the village of Ardsley, NY, was named so by his request because his ancestor, Zechariah Field, was born in East Ardsley, West Riding of Yorkshire, in England. When he retired, he left his New York City financial firm operations to his eldest son, Edward.

Unfortunately, Edward ran the business into the ground within a year and, even worse, after numerous violent outbursts, became institutionalized at an asylum.

The stress of these events worsened the health of aging Cyrus, who died a few months later. Cyrus Field Road in Irvington, where he passed away, is named in his honor.

Due to this string of events, the police then thought the woman found in the Hudson River was not a victim of suicide but instead murder. They theorized that Edward sent the "traveling salesman" to provide a false identification of the deceased body to get them off his trail. While the police suspected Edward's involvement in his seamstress' death, they filed no charges against him.

Soon after, the police focused their suspicions on Edward Allan and Frederick Alz, two brickyard workers, and later a young French man named Duval. It's unclear if the police made any arrests or if the body was ever genuinely identified.

## III. - THE EXPLOSION

On May 19, 1892, a catastrophic event occurred on the Hudson River Railroad in Tarrytown, NY. A wagon load of dynamite exploded at the railway station, killing over thirty men and injuring several dozen more.

Thirty men, primarily Italian laborers, traveled northbound on a flatbed railroad car along the New York Central and Hudson River Railroad tracks. The vehicle contained 500 pounds of dynamite (Ajax Powder) in an open box and some fuse materials. The train was on its way to a construction site at Holmes Point, 300 yards north of where the Tappan Zee Bridge would eventually be.

A spark from the steam locomotive settled on the explosive, and a gigantic blast jolted the community.

The force of the explosion blew the thirty men into fragments. The explosion's force blew the driver and boiler man of another engine in the station into the nearby Hudson River.

The Tarrytown Station suddenly turned into a makeshift emergency field hospital. A hastily assembled rescue squad brought the recovered deceased and injured victims to the Tarrytown station building. The tragedy caused capacity issues at Tarrytown's Provident House Hospital. A special train conveyed victims to Belleview Hospital in New York City.

For days after the explosion, the search continued in the Hudson River for bodies of missing victims.

The explosives involved in the accident were a product of the Rand Drill Company, headquartered on Beekman Avenue in North Tarrytown.

Residents and relatives of the deceased and injured demanded answers. Who was responsible — the railroad workers, the supervisors, or the management?  The coroner's inquest found that all were at fault.

Two years later, Coroner Mitchell, who investigated the catastrophe, filed a lawsuit against a *New York Herald* reporter for slander. Mitchell answered questions from multiple reporters throughout the investigation. But, on one occasion, he refused to give a *Herald* reporter the ante mortem statement of one of the victims, Foreman Finnegan, before he had read it to the jury.

This refusal incensed the reporter to retaliate by writing an article claiming that Coroner Mitchell was intoxicated on the job. The court awarded Mitchell $2,500 in damages, approximately $80,000 today.

The recovered bodies of the disaster were buried, side by side, in a large plot in Sleepy Hollow Cemetery. The New York Central Railroad provided free transportation for attendees of the mass funeral.

## IV – VERY FEW CLUES

In October 1898, three men discovered an unknown man on the brink of the Hudson River lying unconscious. The three men lifted him from the river and took him to the railroad station, where he was conveyed to St. John's Hospital.

Shortly after arriving at the hospital, the man died. An examination of the body showed that both of his arms were bruised near the shoulders and that his body had multiple scars. The victim's injuries suggested foul play.

The police and coroner immediately began an investigation but had little to work with. The victim was about 45 years old, dressed well, and had nothing in his pockets except a pocket knife and a handkerchief with an embroidered "P."

## V - THE LIGHTHOUSE

The lighthouse of Sleepy Hollow is an iconic piece of American history. Its first light shined in 1883, and it still stands today as a testimony to the bravery of its keepers. The first of its ten keepers was Jacob Ackerman, who retired in 1904 after saving 19 lives.

Originally positioned a quarter-mile offshore, the Sleepy Hollow lighthouse now stands closer to the shore, linked by a 100-foot-long footbridge. Its light served as a vigilant warning to sailors until the Tappan Zee Bridge was built in 1955. A lightkeeper resided in the lighthouse until then, and it was rightfully added to the National Register of Historic Places in the 1970s.

The lighthouse's history is not without its tragedies. In March 1974, two brothers, Devon and Harvey Fine, disappeared while fishing on the Hudson River. The police and Coast Guard teamed up to find them, but they only found their small fishing boat floating upside down near the river's east shore, two miles north of the Tarrytown Lighthouse. The motor was missing, and the fate of the brothers remains unknown. The lighthouse still stands as a reminder of the dangers of the river and the bravery of those who have worked to keep others safe.

## VI – THE TAPPAN ZEE BRIDGE

Built to connect Westchester County with neighboring Rockland County, the Tappan Zee Bridge over the Hudson River opened in 1955 after three years of construction.

The six-lane bridge eventually increased to seven and spanned 16,013 feet, the longest in New York State. At its peak, it carried an estimated 135,000 vehicles daily.

The bridge sadly became the site of numerous horrific events. On December 31, 1993, Scott Douglas jumped off the bridge to his death, shortly after murdering his wife, newspaper heiress Anne Scripps.

In 1994, the police identified the body of a man found a half mile south of the Tappan Zee Bridge as an ex-Marine who had been missing from his North Tarrytown boarding room. It remains unknown if the police discovered what transpired.

According to the New York State Thruway Authority, between 1998 and 2008, more than 25 people committed suicide on the Tappan Zee Bridge. In 2007, the NYSTA added multiple phones on the bridge that would connect callers to the National Suicide Prevention Lifeline crisis hotline. Additionally, that year, they added signage with positive messages like "Life is worth living," fencing, and traffic cameras.

In 2009, The History Channel featured the aging bridge, exploiting its infrastructure problems, on their program *The Crumbling of America*. Newspapers referred to it as one of the most dangerous bridges in the country.

In 2013, the New York Thruway Authority began building a new double-span bridge to eventually replace the Tappan Zee, which it completed in 2017. The new bridge, perhaps unpopularly named The Governor Mario M. Cuomo Bridge, opened on August 26, 2017, at an estimated cost of $3.98 billion.

The Tappan Zee Bridge demolition project commenced in November 2017, with the removal of the first steel section of the Rockland County approach. The work continued for several months and involved the removal of the truss sections. In May 2018, the main span, which weighed around 10 million pounds, was taken down, leaving only the east and west approaches.

Initially, the plan was to complete the remaining demolition slowly by dismantling spans piece by piece to minimize environmental impact. However, in September 2018, when the instability of the eastern span was discovered, decision-makers decided to destroy it outright. The explosive demolition of the eastern approach occurred on January 15, 2019, while the western approach was lowered onto a barge on May 12, 2019, and hauled away.

Despite being named the Mario Cuomo Bridge, many locals refer to the bridge as The Tappan Zee or the "The New Tap". More than 100,000 people signed a Change.org petition calling to change the bridge's name, and a Reclaim New York poll of Rockland and Westchester residents found that only 14.7% of respondents supported the Cuomo Bridge name.

After the August 2021 resignation of Governor Andrew Cuomo, who named the bridge after his father, multiple petitions and bills were signed proposing to change the new bridge's name to "The Tappan Zee Bridge", paying homage to the original bridge named after the area's original inhabitants, the Tappan tribe.

# 12.) UP THE RIVER

The expression "up the river" that's used to describe someone in prison or heading to prison derives from New York City convicts serving their sentences in Sing Sing Prison, located up the Hudson River, about 25 miles from the city. The slang expression dates back to 1891, 65 years after Westchester's infamous prison opened its gates.

Sing Sing Prison, located in Ossining, New York, less than four miles from Sleepy Hollow, has a long and storied history dating back to the 19th century. Originally known as the "New York State Prison for Convicts," it was established in 1825 and quickly became one of the most notorious prisons in the United States. Over the years it has housed some of the country's most dangerous criminals.

Angelo Cornetti Sing Sing's tenure began after a drunken brawl resulted in him beating out his wife's brains with a stick. In June 1882, while locked up, he killed Daniel Cash, a fellow convict, by plunging a knife into the unsuspecting victim's jugular vein. The county court in White Plains sentenced him to death by hanging. After his death, his body was placed in a pine box and taken to the county burial ground in Tarrytown.

35-year-old Adrian Braun began his prison sentence in 1898 after beating up his wife. While locked up, she visited him. During the visit, he fatally stabbed her with a potato knife.

Braun had the knife because he worked as a potato peeler in the Sing Sing kitchen, where the correctional officers took Mrs. Braun to visit her husband. Even more shocking is that a few years prior, another inmate named Mangano, also employed in the mess room, stabbed and killed another inmate named Williams with a potato knife.

One of the most talked about inmates at Sing Sing was Charles "Lucky" Luciano, the alleged founder of the modern American mafia. Luciano was sentenced to 30-50 years in Prison in 1936 for his alleged role in the prostitution and narcotics trade. While incarcerated, he allegedly continued to control his criminal empire from behind bars and was eventually released in 1946 after serving only nine years of his sentence.

Other inmates at Sing Sing include notorious bank robber Willie Sutton, who escaped from the prison three times, George "Machine Gun" Kelly, a notorious gangster sentenced to life in prison for kidnapping, and 1970s New York City area serial killer "The Son Of Sam" David Berkowitz.

Sing Sing Prison was also the site of several historic events. In 1915, the prison became the first in the world to use the electric chair as a method of execution. The first inmate to be executed in the electric chair was William Kemmler, who was convicted of murder. The execution was highly controversial, with many people questioning the ethics of using such a brutal method of punishment.

In 1901, Leon Czolgosz was electrocuted for the assassination of U.S. President William McKinley.

Hans Schmidt became the first Catholic priest executed for murder. The police also suspected Schmidt operated a counterfeiting ring with a dentist he was having a secretive homosexual relationship with. The convicted slayer and suspected serial killer met his fate at Sing Sing's electric chair on February 18, 1916, after his conviction for murdering and dismembering a pregnant woman in New York City.

In 1936, local serial killer Albert Fish, rumored to have lived on Buckout Road in West Harrison, was put to death for the cannibal murder of 10-year-old Grace Budd. He was confirmed to have committed at least three murders, but the police suspected his involvement in nine additional murders.

At 65, Fish, known as "The Gray Man," was one of the oldest people ever executed at Sing Sing. Before his execution, he claimed to have murdered more than one hundred people.

In 1953, accused spy couple Julius and Ethel Rosenberg were executed in the electric chair after the couple's conviction for passing nuclear secrets to the Soviet Union during the Cold War, making them the only people in American history to be executed for espionage during peacetime.

Numerous escapes and escape attempts have occurred at the prison. In 1872, when both men and women were housed at Sing Sing, a man escaped in a horse carriage. Fifteen days later, his wife escaped in the same carriage. Almost 50 years later, the woman wrote the warden a letter saying she was living well in Detroit. Included in the letter was a $500 check.

In 1875, five men hijacked a freight train that was passing the prison. After nearly running the train into the Hudson River, they got away. The police caught four, but the fifth successfully got to England, where he opened a pub.

Willie "The Actor" Sutton, who famously robbed banks "because that's where money is" broke out of jail five times in his career. His first escape, in 1932, was from Sing Sing, when he used a makeshift wire ladder to scale an unguarded wall.

In 1983, Sing Sing Prison was the scene of a massive riot that lasted for three days and resulted in the death of two inmates. It's believed that overcrowding and poor living conditions in the prison sparked the riot.

Sing Sing Prison is still in operation, although it has undergone significant changes over the years. The prison now focuses on rehabilitation and education, with programs designed to help inmates prepare for life outside prison.

Sing Sing has long captured the imagination of filmmakers. Numerous films that portray Ossining prison include:

*The Big House* 1930, starring Robert Montgomery.

*Up the River* 1930, starring Spencer Tracy and Humphrey Bogart.

*20,000 Years in Sing Sing* 1932, starring Spencer Tracy, Bette Davis and Arthur Byron.

*Angels With Dirty Faces* 1938, starring James Cagney and Pat O'Brien

*Analyze That* 2002, starring Robert De Niro and Billy Crystal.

Thinly veiled versions of the prison even show up in cartoons: 1950's *Big House Bunny* stars Bugs himself mistakenly tunneling into "Sing Song" prison while trying to evade hunters.

In Episode 24 of the *The Dick Tracy Show* in 1961, the cartoon features the detective with a two-way radio wristwatch to capture two desperadoes who escape from "Sing Song" prison.

 While the prison's history is undoubtedly dark, it is clear that Sing Sing has played an essential role in shaping the American criminal justice system.

# 13.) TARRYTOWN LAKE

Despite the numerous unsolved murders within the confines of Tarrytown and Sleepy Hollow, perhaps the most horrific is one that took place near an unlikely place.

On October 8, 1898, a local Italian man named Giuseppe Gianco informed his wife that he was going hunting in the woods next to Tarrytown Reservoir Lake. However, he did not return home. His absence caused Mrs. Gianco to become worried, and she sent two of their friends to search for him in the woods. The searchers soon returned and informed Mrs. Gianco that they had found a mound of fresh earth in the woods.

 The search party returned in greater force and began to remove the dirt and clay from the mound. In a very short time, they witnessed a horrific sight, making everyone sick. Lying on his side with his hands securely bound behind his back was Giuseppe's dead body.

 Someone had tied his feet together and covered his head with a blue blouse tied around his neck with a rope. Searchers could not locate the gun Mr. Gianco had in his possession when he left home. Mrs. Gianco believed her husband had about a month's worth of wages from his job at the Water Works. But no cash was found.

The police responded immediately and began a thorough investigation as the Coroner ordered Mr. Gianco's body taken to a local morgue.

The police detained six Italian men from the local area who they suspected knew about the murder, but they were uncertain if they had apprehended the killer himself. They discovered that Mr. Gianco had gone to a friend's nearby shanty cabin to play cards with some pals but had gotten into an argument and left. Searchers found Mr. Gianco's body approximately 500 feet away from the shanty cabin.

During questioning, it became revealed that before Mr. Gianco came to the United States, he allegedly slit a man's throat in Italy. The police However, the police suspected the vengeance of the Mafia might be to blame for the murder near Tarrytown Reservoir Lake. By late November, the police issued a $500 reward for any information leading to the arrest of Mr. Gianco's killer. To date, nobody has collected the reward.

In January 1928, a truck driver named Oscar Skilmann saw a man's head bopping up and down through a hole in the ice of the frozen reservoir. The local fire department arrived and retrieved the body of 63-year-old Samuel Raynor, who worked at the Sleepy Hollow Cemetery. Authorities believe Mr. Raynor has stepped on the thin ice, slid some distance, and fallen through.

Despite the gruesome deaths near the Tarrytown Reservoir, by the 1930s, it became a romantic place for young couples to park their cars. In 1931, the Tarrytown police consistently had to shoe away parked cars of teens they referred to as "petters." On one occasion, the police shooed away 15 cars in one night.

In April 1932, a local resident phoned police to say he had found a discarded suit near the water's edge. After dragging the lake, the police recovered the body of an unknown man.

On Christmas Eve 1935, the police searched for a missing 61-year-old resident of the Yonkers County Home. On the day after Christmas, they found him dead, hanging by a sash cord from a limb of a tree next to Tarrytown Reservoir Lake.

In addition to crimes, numerous tragic accidents occurred at the reservoir, including the death of 43-year-old Florida man Lewis Martin in 1970. After losing control of his car, he crashed through a guard rail and landed upside down in the lake.

Scarily, the police remarked that Mr. Martin's death was the fifth fatality on the lakeside road in little more than three months and the eighth in recent years, including four young men from Hastings and Yonkers who were killed early on Christmas morning 1769 when their car plunged into the icy water at the same spot.

# 14.) FIRE BUGS

Mosquitoes are responsible for millions of deaths, especially in countries like Africa, where they afflict people with lethal diseases such as malaria. While not as terrible in the United States, a strange and potentially dangerous mosquito incident occurred in a year when the local mosquito population was abnormally high.

*The Chicago Tribune* may have been the first to break a very unusual story in October 1911 out of Sleepy Hollow. The newspaper reported that mosquitoes on Cortlandt Street in North Tarrytown, NY, have become "gasoline drunkards and are terrorizing the town."

A family of mosquitoes infiltrated James Brady's home, wreaking havoc by consuming gasoline from his car. Their return to the house was disastrous. One mosquito, in a pitiful state, landed on Mr. Brady's nose while he was lighting his pipe, causing a catastrophic explosion that set a mattress ablaze. Mrs. Brady, in her valiant attempt to douse the flames, suffered severe burns, and Mr. Brady's face was also scorched. The neighbors fear this bizarre mosquito behavior could escalate, plunging the town into darkness.

In August, George P. Fox of Elmsford developed an invention to tackle his own mosquito problem. A family trip to Rye Beach, where he watched his children play with balloons, inspired his idea to combat the pesky infestation.

When he got home, he filled one of the balloons with citronella, blew it up, and placed it on a pillow in a dark room. Soon enough, the mosquitoes discovered the balloon and began to attack it. A few minutes later, the balloon exploded with a loud bang. Mr. Fox waited a while before entering the room to allow his invention to work. When he finally went in, he found all the mosquitoes dead.

# 15.) TARRYTOWN ASSEMBLY PLANT

The North Tarrytown Assembly was a General Motors automobile factory operational for 100 years on a 90-acre site on the Hudson River in Sleepy Hollow. During its long history, which started in 1896, the factory experienced several incidents that made headlines in the local and national press.

One of the most notable incidents at the Tarrytown Assembly occurred in 1913 when workers, driven by a shared vision of better working conditions and higher wages, went on strike. The strike, a testament to their unwavering determination, lasted for several weeks and was marked by violence and clashes between the strikers and the police. Eventually, the workers were able to secure some concessions from management, but the strike left a lasting impact on the factory's labor relations.

Another incident that occurred at the Tarrytown Assembly was the explosion of a gas tank in 1928, which killed three workers and injured several others. The blast was caused by a spark from a welding machine, which ignited the gas fumes that had accumulated in the tank. The incident led to a temporary suspension of operations at the factory as investigators worked to determine the cause of the explosion and implement safety measures to prevent future accidents.

In 1930, the Tarrytown Assembly was the site of a major fire that destroyed several buildings and caused millions of dollars in damages. The fire started in one of the factory's paint shops and quickly spread to adjacent buildings, fueled by the flammable chemicals and materials stored on site. Despite the efforts of firefighters, the fire raged for several hours before it was finally brought under control. The incident highlighted the need for better fire prevention and safety measures at the factory.

In the 1950s and 1960s, the Tarrytown Assembly was known for producing iconic American cars, such as the Chevrolet Bel Air and the Pontiac GTO. However, the factory also faced criticism for its environmental impact, as it released large amounts of pollutants into the air and water.

In 1968, three explosions in propane gas storage tanks triggered mass flames that threatened the complex. About a dozen people suffered injuries while fighting the inferno that raged out of control for almost an hour. One witness to the explosions, Larry Clegg of Valley Cottage, said, "I thought an atomic bomb had hit New York. The sky turned bright red, and it spread quickly. My friend and I saw flames shooting 300 feet into the air."

In 1969, a group of activists staged a protest outside the factory, calling for stricter environmental regulations and cleaner production methods.

According to police, in 1973, two men, James Gwynna and Leonard Telesco Jr., both of White Plains, were involved in a car accident in the parking lot at the plant. An argument ensued, and Mr. Telesco allegedly shot and killed Mr. Gwynn and fled. The police eventually arrested Telesco, charging him with murder.

In 1981, six workers filed a $120 million lawsuit against the plant, claiming that they had been permanently poisoned by lead dust from the assembly lines. Their lawyer told the court the workers had suffered vomiting, headaches, blurry vision, and partial paralysis.

In the 1980s and 1990s, the Tarrytown Assembly faced increasing competition from foreign automakers and pressure to reduce costs and improve efficiency.

As a result, General Motors made the heart-wrenching decision to close down the factory in 1996, laying off thousands of workers and ending an era of American manufacturing history. This closure was not just the end of a factory but the end of a chapter in the community's history. The plant was responsible for paying a third of the village's taxes.

After its closure, newspapers reported that the plant agreed that within six years, it would clean up the site where it produced nearly 12 million cars and trucks.

Ten years later, in 2006, *The Journal News* reported that not only had GM failed to clean up the site, but a series of contaminants, including hazardous solvents, methane gas, chromium, and lead, were still buried on the 95-acre industrial site. The site is now home to new million-dollar and-up condos overlooking the Hudson River.

# 16.) PROTEST

On May 30, 1914, eleven men and one woman affiliated with the
Industrial Workers of the World gathered in Tarrytown's public square.
They intended to hold an open-air meeting to protect against a recent
massacre.

The Ludlow Massacre occurred the previous month when the National
Guard, along with the anti-strike military employed by John D.
Rockefeller's Colorado Fuel and Iron Company, attacked a tent colony
of 1,200 people, striking miners and their families in Ludlow,
Colorado. An estimated 21 people, primarily women and children, were
killed during the ensuing violence. People widely believed that
Rockefeller had orchestrated the attack.

The meeting's organizers tried to obtain a permit, but the local
authorities ignored their request. Despite needing to obtain the required
permit, the organizers held their open-air meeting. The police stood
ready to shut it down and arrested each speaker, charged with
disorderly conduct, blocking traffic, and endangering public health.

Becky Edelsohn, a Jewish immigrant from Ukraine, was one of the
known organizers of the Tarrytown meeting. After her arrest for
disorderly conduct, she refused bond. While jailed, *The New York
Times* reported she was the first woman in the United States to attempt
a hunger strike.

She fasted for over 27 days, at which point her friends raised and paid the $300 necessary for her release. By then, two of the Tarrytown protesters had died when a bomb they were building meant for Rockefeller at his Tarrytown estate, Kykuit, went off prematurely in a New York City apartment.

On November 19, 1915, a gardener discovered a powerful dynamite bomb at Cedar Cliff, the Tarrytown estate of John D. Archbold, the president of Standard Oil Company. The police theorized the bomb was planted by anarchists and Industrial Workers of the World members to protest the execution of one of its members in Salt Lake City. The police defused the bomb, set to explode with trip wire across Archbold's driveway before it harmed anyone.

In June 1986, North Tarrytown became the site of what *The Reporter Dispatch* labeled "a full-scale riot." Police from ten departments, some armed with full riot gear and dogs, tried to calm the riot involving an estimated 150 citizens.

The dispute began with an argument between a Black man and a Hispanic man, which escalated after the Hispanic man pulled a knife. The police arrived shortly after, at which point a melee erupted.

At the height of the disturbance, a crowd of 150 people crowded the Sleepy Hollow streets, knocking over garbage cans and screaming at the police.

Police said people threw bottles and rocks from apartment windows and the roof of College Arms, a 200-unit housing project with 1,000 residents on College Ave in the downtown section of the village. Two trash fires and a truck fire also broke out during the riot.

 The police made nine arrests on charges of disorderly conduct, one of which they also charged with possessing ten vials of crack cocaine. After three hours of conflict, the police calmed the riot.

# 17.) SILENT PETE

In 1938, the residents of North Tarrytown were not just intrigued but utterly fascinated by the esoteric man known as Silent Pete. Although his origins are shrouded in mystery, the locals could not resist the allure of this enigmatic figure.

In 1904, the police arrested a 30-year-old man named Morris Conway in Yonkers. Charged with "being a tramp," as per *The Herald Statesman*, he received a thirty-day jail sentence. Two years later, they arrested Conway again. This time on Nepperhan Avenue in Yonkers. They again charged him with "being a tramp" and placed him in county jail for thirty days.

By 1913, Conway relocated three miles away to Bronxville, where, on August 26, he received a five-day jail sentence for vagrancy. The following year, he again caught the attention of the Bronxville police. Only this time, after his arrest, the judge sentenced the homeless man to serve three months in the King's County jail.

By 1931, Conway had relocated to nearby Hastings along the Hudson River. In early December, an automobile struck him as he crossed Warburton Avenue. He sustained only minor injuries, including cuts on his head that doctors treated at St. John's Riverside Hospital in Yonkers.

A few years later, a transformation occurred. Morris Conway became known as Silent Pete by locals and, in 1935, by local newspapers, too. After being arrested, he revealed to the police that he had been headquartering for several years at the Dupont Mansion on South Broadway in Irvington. He said he had always been a welcomed visitor to the rear door of the mansion with a special invitation from Alice Elsie Du Pont, the widow of a recently deceased senator from Delaware and heir to the DuPont fortune, Thomas Coleman DuPont.

However, in 1935, the new owners of the Dupont Mansion were stunned one Sunday morning when they found Silent Pete sleeping in their basement. The police arrived and ushered him out of the mansion.

After adopting his new identity, Silent Pete managed to pique the locals' curiosity. He was often spotted walking between Yonkers and Tarrytown but has yet to speak. Sporting a stubby gray beard with shaggy hair, covered with a dirty brown slouch hat, and black trousers with soleless shoes, his daily routine of silent walks became so mysterious that in 1938, several Westchester newspapers wrote articles about him and interviewed intrigued witnesses.

Tom Matthews, an unemployed man from Dobbs Ferry, told *The Standard Star*,

*"I hear he's rich, all right. I hear he came from a pretty rich family, and when his father died, he was left part of his fortune. But his brother and sister took his dough, so now he walks back and forth, maybe in front of their place. I've seen him for eight or nine years now. I've seen*

*him pass a certain place near Irvington, and he'd look at it and spit sort of mad."*

A Tarrytown counterman said,

*"He's supposed to have been rich once. From what I hear, and I've been around for 12 years now, he was in love with some very rich girl on one of these estates up this way. It must have been 20 or 25 years ago. She's supposed to have thrown him over, so he's been getting back at her by walking up and down past the estate of her husband."*

He's said to walk unevenly but rapidly, stopping to spit every few yards. His hands usually dug into the pockets of his dirty brown overcoat. Sometimes he's seen chewing on cigar butts.

Alois Mater, the operator of a service station at the south end of Hastings, told *The Herald Statesman* he sees Silent Pete "three or four times a day. He always says nothing; he walks mad-like."

Local bakery owner Mrs. Piels observed,

*"He never says anything. He comes here sometimes every day when he has money, and when there is no money, only three or four times a week. I give him food even if he doesn't pay. His only words are 'Anything for a poor man?' when other customers are present. But I heard he's rich."*

A Tarrytown policeman commented, "You know we don't pick him up because we never see him panhandle or anything. He just walks."

Oscar Peterson, a coal dealer, said,

*"I understand he's supposed to have a cave or something up at Sleepy Hollow Cemetery. But I've seen him take a bath at his hut near the Yonkers line. It was a cold day a couple of weeks ago, and he just put some water in an old tub and got in. Gee, it was cold! The guy must be healthy, all right."*

While cemetery directors denied the caves' existence, reporters did get a glimpse of Silent Pete's abode. They described his "ramshackle hut as a hodge-podge of tarpaper strips, wood, tin, and an old brown blanket over a low doorway. The hut is in the center of a sparse clump of trees and refuse-strewn underbrush adjoining the Graham School property. Smoke curls out of a rusty chimney, rising from a crackling old stove inside, and the brush is littered with tin cans.

After his surge of fame in 1938, the trail of Silent Pete runs cold. It remains unknown what the future held for the man who perhaps unknowingly captivated the imaginations of a community.

# 18.) BUSINESS LEGEND

Tom Carvel founded Carvel Ice Cream, one of the most iconic ice cream brands in the United States. He started his business in Hartsdale, New York, in the 1930s, and it quickly grew into a nationwide franchise chain. But what many people don't know is that Carvel also started another food franchise in Dobbs Ferry, New York, called Hubie Hamburgers.

Westchester's Tom Carvel single-handedly revolutionized ice cream by creating soft serve and modernizing desserts. Born in Athens, Greece, in 1906, Athanasios Karvelas moved to the United States as a child with a dream of opening his own business.

He tried his hand as a salesman of radios and automobiles, a test driver for Studebaker, and an auto mechanic. At the age of twenty-six, he was diagnosed with tuberculosis, and his doctors advised him to move out of New York City. Consequently, he borrowed $1,000 from relatives and built a frozen custard trailer.

By 1929, with the Americanized name Tom Carvel, he began selling ice cream from his truck in Hartsdale, but his first big break came a few years later.

On Memorial Day Weekend, 1934, his truck had a flat tire, so he pulled into a parking lot next to a pottery store on Central Avenue and began selling his melting ice cream to vacationers driving by. Tom noticed that the customers preferred the soft melting ice cream to the regular, harder ice cream they were used to.

The pottery store owner allowed Tom to use electricity from his store, so he opened his parked truck for ice cream sales. Within two days, he sold his entire ice cream supply and concluded that he could increase his profits by working from a fixed location. Two years later, Tom purchased the pottery store and converted it into a roadside ice cream stand.

In the 1940s, his wife Agnes operated the Hartsdale store, while Tom traveled to carnivals, selling his frozen treats from a mobile vending vehicle.

In 1936, Tom introduced the "Buy One Get One Free" offer. He also used comic books, ice cream eating contests, and a beauty pageant for young girls called the "Little Miss Half Pint Contest" to attract children to his store.

Tom soon developed a secret soft-serve ice cream formula and new refrigeration machines, which allowed him to franchise his ice cream store. Locations began springing up throughout the area, and Tom increased his advertisements to drive even more business.

Tom's franchising model predated McDonald's. He purchased the Yonkers Motel and revamped it to become The Carvel Inn. There, he operated The Carvel College, where he provided his franchise owners with classes at what became fondly known as "Sundae School."

In 1955, one day, while driving in New York City, Tom heard a radio commercial for a new Carvel store, but the announcer failed to state its exact location. Convinced he could do a better job, he drove to the radio station and re-did the commercial himself. After this incident, he started doing his own commercials on a full-time basis.

Tom Carvel created a distinct style with his garbled delivery and "say it once" philosophy, which emphasized the importance of grabbing people's attention and then letting the product speak for itself. Carvel eventually set up an in-house production studio and advertising agency at the Carvel Inn. He ran television ads for his popular soft-serve ice cream, famous products like Flying Saucers ice cream sandwiches, and iconic ice cream cakes, including Fudgie the Whale, Tom the Turkey, and Cookie Puss.

But Tom didn't stop there. In the 1950s, while living in Ardsley, he started a new food franchise called Hubie Hamburgers. Rumored to be named after Hubert "Hubie" Hause, a former Carvel employee who came up with the idea for a fast food chain that served hamburgers, fries, and milkshakes, its pilot restaurant serving burgers, fries, chicken, and waffles, opened on Saw Mill River Parkway in Dobbs Ferry and several local franchises sprung up in the 1960s around Westchester.

The opening of Hubie's Burgers surprised many. McDonald's CEO Ray Krok allegedly asked Tom if he was interested in setting up the McDonald's chain when the two met in 1956 at a dairy convention. While Tom declined the offer, he later claimed to have given McDonald's permission to use the basic text of his franchise contract and his building design as models.

In 1989, he sold the Carvel Corporation to an international investment company, Investcorp, for more than $80 million. A year later, he died at age 84, having accumulated a fortune conservatively estimated at around $80 million, which triggered a legal battle for the Carvel fortune.

According to reports, after Tom suffered a fatal heart attack, his secretary and the Carvel Corporation's attorney returned to work and allegedly began to take command of Tom's business and personal finances. Tom's widow Agnes claimed she was frozen out of everything, and Tom's niece contended that she was denied millions that her uncle Tom wanted her to receive.

Tom's will reportedly had seven executors, leading to a lengthy ongoing legal battle for the Carvel fortune. Agnes died in 1998, and the secretary and attorney each passed a few years later. In 2007, things took a darker turn when Tom's niece asked for the exhumation of her uncle's body, demanding an autopsy.

She theorized that Tom's secretary and attorney conspired to murder him after Tom had discovered they had embezzled millions from the Carvel corporation.

Before Tom could fire them, he died of a heart attack. Tom's niece hired a private investigator, reportedly believing the pair may have tampered with Tom's heart medicine and forged the death certificate.

A Florida judge ruled against exhuming Tom Carvel's body, and to date, no exhumation has taken place.

The original Carvel location on Central Ave in Hartsdale served its last ice cream cones in October 2008 before closing its doors and being demolished. Shortly after, a new Hibachi restaurant opened on its site.

Operated by Focus Brands, Carvel Ice Cream is still going strong today, with over 320 locations across 19 states and Puerto Rico, including locations in Ardsley, Elmsford, and on North Broadway in Sleepy Hollow. The company also sells its ice cream cakes in more than 8,500 supermarkets. And while Hubie Hamburgers may be a thing of the past, its legacy remains a reminder of Tom Carvel's entrepreneurial spirit and ability to create successful businesses from scratch.

# 19.) HAUNTINGS

Local ghost stories have intrigued Sleepy Hollow residents for generations. Perhaps the first publicized occurrence after Washington Irving's tales of The Headless Horseman and the ghost of Major Andre happened in 1899.

Reports emerged about sightings of a strange woman shrouded in black lurking around the village in the dark. Spooky rumors quietly spread around the neighborhood, including one that said one encounter with the woman supposedly ended with her tossing acid on a victim. Supposedly, by the time the police followed up, the woman in black was gone.

Eventually, North Tarrytown Chief of Police Milton Minnerly interjected himself to solve the mystery of the strange woman in black plaguing the village. A few days later, late one night, two frightened folks came running into the police station, sounding the alarm. The woman in black was out in Beekman Walton's yard. She was still and sitting quietly on Walton's woodpile. Chief Minnerly went to the scene and called out to her, informing the mysterious woman that her days of night-time hijix were finished. Reaching out, he grabbed her arm and attempted to pull her up. The figure crumbled under his grasp, and the seated woman in black turned in a constructed prop of cloth and padding—her loose fabric arm hunt in his hand. Luckily, the police chief had a good sense of humor for the prank.

By the 20th century, rumors of spooky hauntings in multiple locations in and around Sleepy Hollow have emerged.

The King Mansion, a historical landmark on Tarrytown's Sunnyside Lane, is not just a relic of the past, but also a place that promotes its own haunting. The mansion's history is intertwined with the American Tobacco Company, as it was the place where co-founder Benjamin Newtown Duke's daughter, Sybil King, tragically passed away in 1955 on the mansion's second floor.

Sybil King, the wife of Frederick King and daughter-in-law of Thomas King, is said to haunt the King Mansion. Her presence is not just a rumor but a personal experience for many. She has been heard pacing up and down the second-floor hallways, particularly near Room 293, where she took her last breath. Sybil's spirit sometimes manifests as a white apparition or through sounds, orbs, and faint shadows, leaving a lasting impression on guests staying in her former home.

For more, visit TarrytownHouseEstate.com

Several stories circulate at Van Cortlandt Manor in Croton. Among them, is one involving a Hessian soldier who haunts the Prophet's Chambers. The soldier was supposedly wounded during a Revolutionary War battle, and treated in the room, where he later died. This room, steeped in history and tragedy, is a testament to the Manor's past. One of the more common stories is a carriage that is heard pulling to the front of the Manor followed by a flurry of footsteps racing up the main house steps and into the house, echoing the past and keeping the legend alive.

In 1991, Washington Irving's Sunnyside estate workers reported hearing footsteps advancing down a hallway at closing time to the Citizen Register. Irving had desired to return to his home as a friendly ghost.

The Church of St. Barnabas near Sunnyside is also the site of alleged hauntings. One former occupant supposedly matched a photo of a 19th-century pastor's family member to a female apparition who used to knit from one of the home's rocking chairs. In 2000, a group of men installing a new organ claimed to have seen the ghost of the church's first pastor.

Built in 1885 by local chocolate manufacturer William L. Wallace, the Tarrytown Music Hall has entertained wealthy families like the Rockefellers and Vanderbilts at lavish balls, flower shows, and concerts. In 1901, it was one of the first theaters to show a new form of entertainment called motion pictures.

With its distinctive two-and-a-half-story structure, the Tarrytown Music Hall proudly holds the title of the oldest theater in Westchester County that is still in use as a theater. Its age and unique status add to its rumored hauntings' intrigue, earning it a spot on The Haunted History Trail of New York. The Gotham Paranormal Research Society, a team of dedicated investigators, has delved into the mysteries of the Music Hall several times. Their findings have been nothing short of fascinating, with intriguing Electronic Voice Phenomena audio recordings and Electromagnetic Field readings consistently pointing to the presence of the supernatural.

Renowned master storyteller Jonathan Kruk, featured on the Travel Channel and known for his annual one-person Legend of Sleepy Hollow shows at The Old Dutch Church, offers recurring Ghost Tours of the Music Hall.

Visit TarrytownMusicHall.org to learn more.

# 20.) SLEEPY HOLLOW CEMETERY

The Old Dutch Church in Sleepy Hollow, New York, has a rich history dating back to the 17th century. Originally built in 1685, the church has been rebuilt and restored several times. It is located in the heart of Sleepy Hollow, a famous village for its connection to the supernatural and the legend of the Headless Horseman. This legend, popularized by Washington Irving's 'The Legend of Sleepy Hollow,' adds a layer of intrigue and mystery to the village's history, especially as Irving not only mentions The Old Church in his famous tale but he is  also buried in the neighboring Sleepy Hollow Cemetery.

The Old Dutch Church played an essential role in the American Revolution, serving as a hospital and a barracks for soldiers. It was also a prominent meeting place for the Patriots fighting for independence. Many of the soldiers buried in the adjacent Sleepy Hollow Cemetery were Revolutionary War veterans.

 The Sleepy Hollow Cemetery, established in 1849 near The Old Dutch Church, is a testament to tranquility and beauty. Its serene setting, nestled in nature, is the final resting place of many illustrious Americans, each with their own unique contributions to the nation. Among them are Andrew Carnegie, the renowned steel magnate and philanthropist; William Rockefeller, the famous co-founder of Standard

Oil; and Walter Chrysler, the innovative founder of the Chrysler Corporation. Their legacies continue to inspire and shape the world we live in today.

Andrew Carnegie led the expansion of the American steel industry in the late 19th century and became one of the wealthiest Americans in history. Known for his philanthropy, he funded the construction of thousands of libraries nationwide and donated millions of dollars to various causes, leaving a lasting impact on education and culture. Carnegie died in 1919 and was buried in the Sleepy Hollow Cemetery.

William Rockefeller, the younger brother of John D. Rockefeller, was a successful businessman and philanthropist who played a significant role in the growth of the Standard Oil Company. After a long and prosperous life, William passed away in Tarrytown, New York, on June 24, 1922, at age 81. He was buried at the historic Sleepy Hollow Cemetery in the same town where he had lived for many years.

William Rockefeller's funeral was momentous, drawing in many prominent figures of the era. The funeral service, held at the Union Church of Pocantico Hills, was a testament to the Rockefeller family's influence and was filled with mourners, a testament to William's impact on their lives.

After the service, he was interred in a family plot in a peaceful corner of The Sleepy Hollow Cemetery surrounded by trees and shrubs. His tombstone is a simple but elegant marker inscribed with his name and birth and death dates. Tourists and history buffs interested in the Rockefeller legacy often visit.

Automobile pioneer Walter Chrysler founded the Chrysler Corporation in 1925. He was known for his innovative designs and his commitment to quality. Chrysler died in 1940 at age 65.

George Washington Hill was a business magnate who made his fortune in the tobacco industry. He was a controversial figure in his time, known for his aggressive marketing tactics and battles with the government over taxes and regulations. Hill's career included being the first to market cigarettes to women. Hill owned a large estate in Irvington and died in 1946. In 1955, his former Mamaroneck Avenue estate in White Plains burned in a fire, rumored to have been started by a non-fully-extinguished lit cigarette.

In addition to these famous burials, the Sleepy Hollow Cemetery is home to many other notable figures, including Samuel Gompers, the founder of the American Federation of Labor, businesswoman Elizabeth Arden, one-armed war veteran Isaac Martling, and real estate mogul Harry Helmsley who built a company that became one of the biggest property holders in the United States.

The Old Dutch Church and the Sleepy Hollow Cemetery are popular tourist attractions, drawing visitors from all over the world, many visiting the gravesite of Washington Irving.

The church, still an active congregation, holds regular services, inviting visitors to participate in its ongoing history. Meanwhile, the cemetery offers tours and special events throughout the year, providing a unique opportunity to connect with the past.

One of the area's most popular attractions is its recurring spooky-themed Halloween hayride. The attraction transports guests from nearby Sleepy Hollow High School past the Old Dutch Church and Sleepy Hollow Cemetery, encountering appearances from various costumed characters, including a particular horseman.

117

Additional books from the *Nightmarish Neighborhood* series are available now on Amazon and BarnesAndNoble.com.

For more info, please visit:   RightOnDudes.com

www.ingramcontent.com/pod-product-compliance
Lightning Source LLC
Chambersburg PA
CBHW022158150726
47992CB00002B/846